D0915892

double time

ALSO BY JANE ROPER

Eden Lake

double time

how i survived—and mostly thrived—through the first three years of mothering twins

JANE ROPER

St. Martin's Press
New York

www.stmartins.com

ISBN 978-0-312-55223-7 (hardcover)
ISBN 978-1-250-01491-7 (e-book)

First Edition: May 2012

10   9   8   7   6   5   4   3   2   1

FOR ELSA AND CLIO, OF COURSE

Introduction

When I found out I was pregnant with twins, I was, to put it mildly, terrified. I immediately, desperately scoured bookstores and Web sites for firsthand accounts of what it was like to have and raise two babies at once.

And although I found several straight-up how-to books and a couple of blogs (mom blogging hadn't yet become quite the phenomenon it is now), I didn't find what I was really after: a window into what my life might be like once these two babies were born. I wanted confirmation that, yes, I could manage it and, yes, there were things about twins that were absolutely wonderful. I also wanted reassurance that, no, I wouldn't lose myself completely in the process. I would still be a professional, a writer, a woman—not just a Mother of Twins with a capital *M* and *T.*

I wrote this book in an attempt to provide all of the above to people who have or are about to have twins. Because I'm guessing there are a few people out there who might want that glimpse, and that reassurance, as badly as I did.

I wrote this book for another reason, too: a year after my girls were born, I began having episodes of clinical depression more severe than any I'd experienced before. Now, faced with the challenge of trying to mother my twin toddlers while struggling just to get through the days, I went searching again, this time for books or blogs or *anything* about parenting and depression. I found a few clinical-type resources. Some accounts of depression immediately postpartum. And some really awesome poetry. But nothing that quite spoke to what I was going through.

I hope that this book's secondary subject—my journey through depression and back out again—helps show fellow depression sufferers that they're not alone and that it is possible to manage depression and parenthood. Provided you do whatever it takes to get better.

But know this: my story isn't extraordinary on either front. Having twins isn't exactly surviving abuse or battling cancer or living in a war zone. With the rate of twin births climbing in the United States and throughout the developed world, it's not that uncommon anymore, either. You have to rate at least quads, maybe even quints, for your own reality TV show.

As for my depression, yes, it got pretty bad at times. It disrupted my life and my relationships. But I was never hospitalized, never suicidal. I've got an excellent support network of family and friends, good health insurance, and financial security—a best-case scenario for someone with mental illness.

So this isn't quite what you'd call triumph of the human spirit in the face of impossible odds. It's just me—an unfamous, comfortably middle-class, working mother of twins with a tendency toward sarcasm, corniness, and clinical depression—sharing my story in the hopes that it will help some people out there feel a little less terrified, a little less alone, as they face the challenges on the road ahead. And in hopes that, like me, they will find that for every moment of frustration and exhaustion there are double the moments of sheer joy.

I

It got suddenly very quiet in the exam room.

I was just over six weeks pregnant, at the fertility clinic for a follow-up ultrasound to make sure my pregnancy was on the right track: not ectopic, not an empty egg sac, not a false alarm.

There were five of us crammed into the tiny room: a young doctor doing the ultrasound; the senior doc who'd overseen my fertility treatments; a nurse; my husband, Alastair; and me—lying on the table with my feet in stirrups and an ultrasound wand plunged up into my ladyparts.

Seconds earlier, the doc wielding that wand had been providing a running commentary on what we were seeing on the screen—a friendly little tour of my reproductive organs: "Right here's your cervix, here are your ovaries, and this, you can see, is your uterus—nice thick lining there—and right here . . . we should be able to see the . . . uh . . ."

There was (forgive me) a pregnant pause.

I held my breath and waited for the bad news: the embryo was gone or dead or implanted in the wrong place. This was going to be just one more disappointment, one more defeat. Who was I to think that my subpar reproductive system could actually sustain a pregnancy? And what had we been thinking, telling our parents the good news the same day we got a positive pregnancy test? Stupid, stupid, stupid.

The doctor now maneuvered the wand until it felt like it was horizontal inside me.

"OK, so," he finally said. "We appear to be looking at two pregnancies."

Two pregnancies? I thought. What the hell does that mean? How can one person have two pregnancies at the same time? Unless . . .

"It's twins?" I said, idiotically.

"Yep," said the doc. "Congratulations."

I looked up at Alastair, dumbstruck. I might have smiled a little, in a "holy crap, can you believe it?" sort of way. Mostly, though, I was searching for reassurance, proof that he didn't hate me for this. After all, it was my lazy ovaries, and their subsequent dosing up with fertility drugs, that had gotten us into this. And anyway, why had I been so eager to start down the road of fertility treatments? We'd only been trying for a year before we went the intervention route. We could have kept at it a little longer on our own. It might have happened.

Looking at him, I wondered if he was thinking all of these same things, hoping he wasn't. But I've known the man since I was eighteen years old, and there are still times when I find his face difficult to read. For a man as funny and often downright silly as Alastair is, his smiles are surprisingly few and far between. And although his eyes have an impressive capacity for twinkling—

one of the qualities that drew me to him in the first place—his poker face is equally good.

He gave me what could be vaguely interpreted as a smile, squeezed my hand, and then squinted back at the ultrasound screen.

The older doctor, who had been sitting silently on a stool near the sink this whole time, finally spoke. "It's really something, isn't it?" His smile was thoughtful but smug, as if he'd known this all along. And maybe he had; my HCG numbers from the blood pregnancy test a few weeks earlier had been through the roof. Come to think of it, maybe that's why he was here in the first place.

I looked back at the ultrasound screen, and there they were: two little black beans in a field of fuzzy gray, each with a small white spot in its center where a heart would soon grow. Something about the fact that there were two of them made them seem more alive, more human, than I think would have been the case if there were only one. They were hanging out together. Keeping each other company. How strange. How utterly surreal.

The doc at the controls hit a button and the image froze. "We'll give you that shot to take home as a souvenir," he said. Then he looked over my shoulder at Alastair and said, very seriously, "Are you OK? Do you need to sit down? You look kind of pale."

"No, I'm OK," Alastair said, this time smiling for real. "But you're sure there are only two in there, right?"

Before we left the exam room, the doctors asked if we had any questions.

Any questions? I had about a million, tumbling and vaulting through my brain: Can my (rather petite) body handle this? Will I be OK? Will *they* be OK? What if they're born premature, with all kinds of terrible complications? And while we're at it, how are we going to afford this? Am I going to have to quit my job?

Are our careers / social life / sex life over? And, dear God, what if I just don't have what it takes to be a mother of twins? I'd been nervous enough about the prospect of one baby, but this? This was ridiculous.

But the only question I could manage to choke out was: Could I really not eat cold cuts? Because of the bacteria or nitrates or whatever the reason was you weren't supposed to eat them when you were pregnant? Because I ate a lot of turkey sandwiches.

"You're probably OK with turkey," the younger doc said. "But I'd stay away from the more processed stuff, like olive loaf."

The older doctor nodded sagely. "I'd definitely stay away from olive loaf."

After shuffling numbly out of the clinic, squeaking our way over the shining, high-wax floors to the banks of elevators—I wondered how many other couples had made the same, dazed shuffle under similar circumstances—we had breakfast in the cafeteria on the first floor. Alastair got a very large plate of eggs, bacon, and other classic oh-my-God-I'm-having-twins comfort food. I got a blueberry yogurt and a decaf coffee. We sat across from each other at a wobbly table, silent.

I believe I eventually said something profound and articulate along the lines of "wow."

What else could I say? This was far too much of a shock, far too much to process at once.

Alastair, God bless him, was thinking much more clearly, and in a decidedly more positive vein. "You know, I've always worried," he began, "that if we had one baby, we might never get around to having another one. We'd get in the mind-set of having a two- or three-year-old and wouldn't want to go back to the whole baby thing again. Or we'd be busy with our work and the timing would never be right."

Alastair is an only child who'd always wished he had a sibling. Like me, he wanted very much for us to have two children.

"And," he went on—he'd clearly done a lot of thinking in the elevator and/or while waiting for his eggs—"there would have been the fertility issues, too. We might have had trouble getting pregnant a second time. Or what if we had one baby first, and then had twins after that? That would be pretty tough."

This way, he reasoned, we got our two children in one fell swoop. And yes, it would be hard, especially at first, but we'd do it. "To be honest," he said, "I think part of me was hoping we'd end up with twins."

No part of me had been. But I nodded, hmmed, and conceded all his points. They were good ones. They made absolute sense. Yes, yes, yes, this is good, I told myself. It's better than good. I'm excited. No, really, I am. We're going to have two beautiful babies. It's gonna be fine. It's gonna be fine. It's gonna be *great*.

And anyway, who was I to be choosy? For a while it looked like I wasn't going to be able to get pregnant at all, let alone twice at the same time.

We had started trying a year and a half earlier, not long after we moved back to Boston after a two-year stint in Iowa, where I got my MFA in fiction writing—along with a hankering for a baby. The urge wasn't so much physical (no tingling ovaries) as psychological: I started feeling maternal around babies, instead of just vaguely amused and slightly annoyed. I felt a growing sense of fondness and protectiveness for children. A few friends and acquaintances were starting to have babies, and when I held them, it felt more natural and more satisfying than it ever had before. For the first time, I could imagine myself as a mother.

Meanwhile, I was starting to feel like something was missing—this despite the fact that life was actually pretty terrific. I was working part-time as an advertising copywriter, as I'd done before grad school, while also working on a novel. Alastair, who's a singer-songwriter and musician, played on the folk scene in Boston and beyond, with occasional brief tours elsewhere in the United States and in Europe. He also worked part-time teaching guitar lessons. It was a lovely, semi-bohemian sort of life, full of books and music and friends and wine. A lot of wine.

But at just shy of thirty-two, I was getting a bit bored with the total freedom of our lives. We were responsible for no one but ourselves, and one very low-maintenance cat. Holidays rang a bit hollow, and weekend days began to feel a tad roomy. One Saturday morning I had the distinct and very strange feeling of waking up and thinking to myself, "Where are the kids?" As if we really ought to have some, and we should all be going to a museum or on a hike or something. Or cleaning out the garage. You know, family stuff.

Not that we were unhappy by any means. And, granted, there were some conditions in our lives that weren't ideal for starting a family. Neither of us was making a whole lot of money, nor had either of us actually "made it" in our respective artistic fields (whatever that means). The apartment we lived in was drafty and inefficiently laid out, and I would have had to sacrifice my office to use as a nursery, which I wasn't thrilled about. Plus, our landlord, a preternaturally energetic massage therapist and cycling fanatic, liked to tinker with his bikes in the basement at all hours while singing along in full voice to, among other things, gangsta rap. Many a morning we woke up to a gleeful string of F-bombs, bitches, and hos.

But we ultimately decided, as many couples do, that there would never be a completely ideal time to have a baby. I had a feeling it might not be easy for us, given the fact that my periods tended to be infrequent when I wasn't regulating them with oral contraceptives. If we wanted to have two kids while I was still firmly in my thirties, I thought we might as well get the show on the road.

Still, our attitude was, I'd go off the pill and it would happen when it happened. Maybe sooner, maybe later. No pressure. We weren't really *trying*. Just not *not* trying.

Ha.

Is anyone actually that chill about having a baby? Maybe they are. But in my experience—and that of my friends who are psychotic overachieving types like me—once I was in unprotected sex mode, I wanted to be pregnant more than anything in the world. It needed to happen *Right Now*. And if it didn't (and it didn't), then clearly we were barren and would never have a baby, so we might as well start saving for plane tickets to China, because we were going to have to adopt. No question.

I'd hoped that after ten-plus years on the pill, my cycles might have been whipped into shape, and I'd be more regular. But, well, no. I didn't get my first period until almost three months after I went off the pill. After that, they came anywhere from five to nine weeks apart. (Yes, this is one of those oversharing kinds of books.)

I did the charting thing—taking my temperature in the mornings and watching for various signs of ovulation—with the hope that maybe I could crack my body's crazy code and figure out what, exactly, was going on. But month after month went by with none of the temperature spikes that are supposed to happen before ovulation, no positive results on ovulation-predictor tests, and definitely no positive pregnancy tests.

Just lots and lots of dutiful sex, on the off chance that maybe, *maybe*, we'd just happen to be doing it when an egg decided to drop.

You can only have so much sex and actually enjoy it. We sure did give it the old college try, though. By which I mean that college was the last time we'd had so much sex. But this wasn't nearly as much fun.

It wears on you, not being able to conceive once you've set your mind to it. With every month that passed, every stick I peed on to no avail, my urge for a baby grew keener, and my faith in my body weaker. Suddenly I heard my biological clock not so much ticking as blaring the theme song from *Jeopardy!* I began to panic: how was I going to have the two healthy kids I wanted while I was still young and vigorous? I was practically *forty!!* (Quick reminder: I was thirty-two.)

Meanwhile, every other woman in the universe was getting pregnant, from Britney Spears to teenage meth addicts to an infuriating number of my female friends.

Seeing a baby or pregnant woman would frequently bring tears to my eyes. I felt as if the future I wanted for myself—the future I could imagine so clearly and that had seemed so natural and inevitable—was being kept from me behind a locked door.

After about a year of trying—during which time we bought and moved into a much more family-friendly house, gangsta-rap free and complete with small backyard—I decided it was time to go to a fertility clinic and see if we could figure out what the heck was going on with my reproductive system.

The tests revealed that I wasn't doing a whole lot of ovulating. Which is problematic when you're trying to make a baby. The doctors were optimistic, however, that with help from ovulation drugs, in combination with intrauterine insemination (the official, medical name for the turkey baster method) to get the sperm a little bit closer to the target, we had a very good chance of conceiving. We were fortunate enough to live in the great Commonwealth of Massachusetts, where fertility treatments are covered up to a certain point (is it any wonder we have the highest twin birthrate of any state?), and so we decided to go for it.

Before we started trying to have a baby, Alastair and I were always of the mind that we'd adopt if we couldn't manage to have a biological child. Back before we got married, when we were in our early twenties, we even talked about adopting instead of having a baby of our own. Alastair, in particular, felt that in a world with a burgeoning population and limited resources, where there were always children in need of loving homes, it was the more responsible and generous thing to do. But it's easy to talk in the idealistic abstract when you're nowhere close to having kids. And it's easy to say you don't feel strongly about having a biological child before you actually start wanting to have one.

Infertility sucks. And we only got a small dose of it: I was pregnant less than two years after we started trying. Which is nothing compared to the many years that some couples struggle.

I hope you'll pardon me while I interrupt this memoir with a brief public service announcement: if you know someone who is having difficulty conceiving, be kind to them. Do not say, "You can always adopt!" or "Have you tried taking X vitamin/mineral/ herb supplement?" or "Maybe it's just not meant to be." Just tell them you're really sorry and that it must be so difficult. It is.

. . .

Something else happened in the midst of our conception quest: I tried to stop taking the antidepressants I'd been on since I was twenty-three.

My depression had never been what I'd call severe. I was never hospitalized or suicidal, and I'd never felt so awful that I couldn't drag myself out of bed in the mornings. But it was bad enough that when I was having a depressive spell, it interfered with my ability to work productively and handle social interactions with some modicum of normality.

The first time it happened was when I was twenty-three. I was living with a couple of roommates in a shabby but charming Somerville double-decker, loving my job as the assistant to the president and creative director of a smallish Boston ad agency— the same one I would return to seven years later, on a part-time basis, when we moved back from Iowa. My boss, generous and mentorly, helped me find opportunities to try my hand at copywriting, and I had dreams of becoming an advertising superstar, racking up awards and big bucks.

When I was in college, I had majored in anthropology and imagined I'd go into international development, or some sort of philanthropic career path. As in, nothing remotely like advertising. But at the nonprofit I worked at right after college, as an administrative assistant in the fund-raising department, my favorite parts of the job were the opportunities I had to write and be creative—working on event invitations and postcards, letters, and the like. Meanwhile, my father, a marketing consultant, had been urging me to talk to one of his contacts at a local ad agency— one he noted as being particularly cool and nontraditional, in a former warehouse in South Boston—just to get a taste of another potential career path out there, one where I might be able to put my creative abilities to work. I resisted; *advertising?* Why didn't I just shake hands with the devil while I was at it? But I was feeling increasingly frustrated and unsatisfied with my current job and decided to go for it. Six weeks later, I had a job offer and, without a second thought, hopped over to the dark side. And loved it.

So it didn't make any sense to me when, about seven months into the job, I started feeling edgy and detached. I felt oversensitive and easily offended, inclined to take things personally in a way I didn't normally. I began finding it more difficult to concentrate, and my drive and enthusiasm for my work vanished. In fact, I didn't feel like doing much of anything. I was tired and lethargic. It was as if I was looking out at the world from behind a dirty window.

And yet, nothing was *wrong.* On an intellectual level, I knew that I still liked my job and my life circumstances. Alastair and I had recently gotten back together after a tumultuous two on-again off-again years, during which we tried to figure out whether or not our college romance was meant to survive for the long haul. It was a painful transition. But things were solid now—in fact, we felt almost like we were falling in love all over again. Though we hadn't spoken it aloud, I think we both knew we were together to stay.

And as for any deep-seated, psychological issues that might be at the core of these blues I was having? I couldn't imagine what they might be. (And why would they flip on, like a switch, for no reason?)

I waited for the funk to pass; I tried eating better and exercising more. I tried doing yoga. I even bought a couple of aromatherapy candles (proof that I was, clearly, desperate). But I couldn't kick it.

It was Alastair who urged me to see a doctor.

We were taking one of our typical weekend walks—the kind
that sometimes lasted all day: we would start out from his apartment or mine, usually wending our way to Harvard Square, stopping at shops along the way. Buying lunch. Perhaps catching a
spontaneous matinee movie. Sometimes we'd walk ourselves over
the Charles and all the way into Boston, maybe have dinner, and
then take the T back to Somerville.

On this day, though, we didn't make it far before I wanted to
turn back. I didn't feel like I could walk at full speed, and I wasn't
having fun. All I wanted was to take a nap.

He tried to convince me to keep going. "Walking's good for
you. I don't think it makes sense to wallow."

"I'm not going to wallow," I snapped. "I just want to be alone."
I immediately regretted my tone, and added, "I'm sorry. It's not
you at all. Everything's fine. I'm happy with us. I just don't feel
good."

"OK, fine," he said.

"Please don't be mad at me."

"I'm not," he said, after a pause and a sigh. "I'm just disappointed. I thought we were having a nice day."

"I'm sorry," I said. And I was. But I felt too tired, too gloomy
to keep going.

We walked slowly home, and as he tucked me into bed—it
was a relief to be back in my own room—he said, "I think this
is depression."

I protested that I didn't feel sad; I just felt . . . blah.

"But low-grade depression can feel like that," he insisted. "I
think you should talk to a doctor. It may be something that
medication could help with."

"It's not *that* bad," I said. "Not like what you had."

A contributing factor to why Alastair and I had had a roller coaster of a relationship over the previous two years was the fact that he was depressed. Of course, neither of us fully realized this in the midst of it. He attributed his low mood, lack of interest or motivation, and social anxiety to the stress of transitioning to life after college, and to uncertainty about our relationship. Which was, no doubt, at least part of the issue. But when he got to the point where he could barely function, he saw a psychiatrist. He got on medication. And not long after that, he felt like himself again.

The change was dramatic: I remember seeing him for the first time in several months—he was about to leave on a trip to Southeast Asia with his father and wanted to talk with me before he left—and being amazed. My God, I thought, here was the person I'd fallen in love with in college, twinkling eyes and all. Where had he been all this time?

"You might not be as severely depressed as I was," Alastair said to me now. "But I wasn't either at first."

"But, ugh. I don't want to take medication," I said. "It feels like wimping out."

"Look, baby, if you were diabetic, you'd take insulin. If you had epilepsy, you'd take whatever people with epilepsy take. It's the same thing."

Maybe. But I still saw medication as being something for people with *severe* depression. I was still working, still eating. Still showering regularly.

But I agreed to make an appointment.

The psychiatrist I saw a couple of weeks later—young, kind, and bearded—concurred with Alastair's armchair diagnosis and prescribed a low dose of Prozac. "All the things you're describing," he said, "losing interest, having trouble concentrating, sleeping more than usual, feeling like you're looking at the world from behind a dirty window—they're classic signs of depression."

I agreed to give the medication a try. To my delight, within a little over a week, I felt significantly better. And within three weeks, I was back in business.

Just over a year later, I tried, under my doctor's supervision (and against Alastair's protests), tapering off the drugs to see if I could manage without them. Apparently sometimes after an initial course of antidepressants, some people are fine and don't need them anymore. But within two months, I was depressed again. Back on the juice I went.

And yet, because I can be incredibly stubborn, I tried to go antidepressant-free eight years later, when we started trying to conceive. I knew that the risks to unborn babies from Prozac were minimal, to the extent that they had been studied. I knew it was one of those risk-benefit equations: does the emotional harm of my going off antidepressants outweigh the benefits to the fetus of my not being on them?

But I still wanted to see if I could wean myself off the damned stuff and avoid exposing my future offspring to selective serotonin reuptake inhibitors.

My psychiatrist—a different one now, older but also bearded— was skeptical, but he understood my concerns and helped me taper gradually off the drugs. For a couple of months, I felt fine. I'd taken the training wheels off my bike and—behold—I could ride without them.

But pretty soon, that bike started veering off the pavement. I felt anxious and irritable, and I teared up at completely random moments, like, say, when I saw a stop sign that struck me as particularly poignant. I kept telling myself that I was OK. It really *was* a poignant stop sign. But it wasn't long before I slid right back into the dim, depressive zone I knew so well and detested so completely.

I had hoped that perhaps after so many years on Prozac, my body might have healed itself—in the same way I'd hoped birth control pills might have healed my malfunctioning menstrual cycles. But pharmaceuticals generally do not heal; they only keep the symptoms at bay. They channel your neurons and hormones in more desirable directions, like tiny traffic cops. Take away the cops, and you get a pileup.

I couldn't stand the thought of being depressed while I was pregnant. I did not want to miss out on what was going to be, I hoped, one of the most meaningful experiences of my life. And I knew that I couldn't—simply could not—be the mother I wanted to be if I was depressed.

My father suffers from depression, too. For a time, when I was in my teens, his depression was severe—so severe that sometimes when I came downstairs in the morning to eat breakfast before school, he would be in a fetal position on the couch, wincing aloud, nearly weeping, from the pain of this thing inside him. And nothing that any of us did—pep talks, comforting words, hugs, jokes—seemed to have any effect. I hated that feeling of helplessness.

Starting then, I resolved not to bring the burden of depression into my children's lives if I could help it. I did not want that damned, dark beast breathing down my loved ones' necks.

And so I went back on medication.

Fast-forward a few weeks, and I feel like myself again.

Fast-forward a little more than a year, and I am elated: I wake up on a Wednesday morning, just shy of two weeks after our most recent round of fertility drugs and IUI, my breasts wonderfully, auspiciously sore, and take a home pregnancy test. Two pink lines appear. Hallelujah.

2

After my two best friends from high school (to whom I tell absolutely everything), my mother was the first person I told that I was having twins, the same day as the big, revelatory ultrasound.

I was teaching a "jump-start your novel" writing course for adults in the evenings that spring and came to class that night feeling distracted and disoriented (not to mention bloated). *I'm pregnant with twins,* I'd been saying to myself all day, trying to make it feel more real. *How could I possibly be pregnant with twins?*

As I stood at the chalkboard drawing a diagram of the typical arc of a novel—slow build, rising conflict and tension, dramatic peak, resolution, and denouement—all I could think was, "Gee, that looks like a diagram of a woman hugely pregnant with twins, lying on her back."

I felt the urgent need to tell someone else about this new reality of my life, if for no other reason than to help get myself used to it. I also needed some reassurance that everything was going to be OK—that this was, in fact, a good thing.

The class was held at a school in the heart of Cambridge's busy, quirky, and slightly sketchy Central Square. There was a warm, misty rain falling, but I went outside, ducked into a doorway, and, pressing one finger to my ear to block out the sounds of traffic and sirens and two drunken men arguing nearby, called my mother.

"So," I said, "we had another ultrasound today and . . ."

"You're having twins," she cut in.

"How did you know?"

"I don't know. I just had a feeling this was going to happen . . ." She said it in a "yikes" kind of way. Not exactly comforting.

I felt the push of tears in my throat. "Well, it's not what we wanted. At all. But it's two and through, at least."

What I had always hoped for was to have two children spaced a reasonable two to four years apart. I wanted them to have what I did (and still do with my younger brother)—a sweet and supportive big/little sibling relationship. God knows I didn't want it to happen all at once.

It occurred to me that maybe my mother felt the same way about having her first grandchildren. She and my father had been eager for Alastair and me to have kids, but I'm sure that twins didn't figure into their grandparenting dreams. I felt suddenly guilty for not giving them what they'd hoped for.

And then my mother said, "I think it's kind of cool, Janey." The "yikes" was gone from her voice now, and to my relief she sounded much more momlike and nurturing.

I wiped away a couple of tears. "It's probably not what you were hoping for."

"Well, no, I guess it's not what I was expecting. But that's OK. We'll welcome them to our family, and love them, and I think in some ways it'll be fun. There'll always be a baby to hold!"

I got the sense that she was trying to convince herself at the same time she was trying to convince me. But I liked hearing her refer to her future grandchildren as "them." I had a brief vision of the guest room in my parents' house, with its twin beds. I could vaguely imagine two children—two future members of the family—sleeping in them.

For the moment, I was reassured. But it didn't last long.

A week later, I had yet another follow-up ultrasound. I didn't ask any questions about cold cuts this time. This time I asked what the chances were that both embryos would remain viable.

I knew, from the copious amounts of reading I'd done on fertility and early pregnancy, that a surprising number of single pregnancies actually start out as twin ones. But the mothers and their doctors never know it, since the first ultrasounds aren't typically performed until after the second embryo (or fetus, after eight weeks) ceases to be viable and is absorbed into the woman's body. It's called vanishing twin syndrome.

Was I asking about this because I didn't want to get used to the idea of twins if there was a good chance that one of those little beans on the screen was going to disappear? Or was I asking because I was hoping one *would* disappear?

I'm ashamed to admit that it was a little bit of both.

There was so much about the prospect of twins that I feared. I worried that I might love one baby more than the other. I worried that I wouldn't have the time or energy to bond with them the way mothers bond with a single baby, because I'd be so busy juggling the two of them. I worried that I'd resent them because they weren't the single child I'd hoped for. I even found myself, in the early weeks and months of my pregnancy, mourning, a little, the one baby that I thought I'd have. As if I'd known him (or her), and he'd gone. Vanished, replaced by this little pair of strangers.

I had known all along, of course, that twins were a possibility. But even in the midst of using injected fertility drugs (also known as—tee hee—gonadotropins), which came with a 15–20 percent chance of a multiple pregnancy, I'd assumed I would beat the odds. What was a 15–20 percent chance in the face of my 100 percent certainty that I just wasn't a twins kind of *person*? As much I wanted to be a mother, I knew that I wasn't meant to be an übermother—the kind to whom mothering comes as naturally as breathing and who throws herself 100 percent into rearing her children in the infant and toddler years, to the exclusion of career. But this sort of all-encompassing parenthood seemed unavoidable with twins.

We'd expected that neither of us would be able to spend as much time on our "art" (his music, my writing) once a baby—one baby—came around. As the primary breadwinner, I'd have to keep working, and Alastair would do the majority of the weekday child care. But I hoped I would still be able to sneak in an hour or two here and there to peck at my novel.

With twins, though, the whole thing seemed certain to go to pot. I'd never write another word for at least a couple of years, maybe more. My literary life, such as it was, would be completely crowded out by dirty diapers, soggy Cheerios, and screaming in stereo.

Even the prospect of going back to work seemed iffy. Sure, lots of mothers worked. But did they have twins? And were their husbands the child care plan? I knew Alastair was going to be a great dad, and had no doubt that he was capable of taking care of one baby while I worked. But could he handle two? And could we afford a sitter or nanny to help out?

We tried to think of areas where we could trim expenses, but we weren't exactly living large. We figured movies and dinners out would take care of themselves. I would try to refrain from buying new clothes, but who knew what crazy things this pregnancy might do to my body? The only things we could come up with to cut were cable, Netflix, and wine. So basically all of our evening entertainment options, not counting Scrabble and sex, that didn't require hiring a sitter. And we'd probably be too tired for sex anyway.

Once, early in my second trimester, I ran into an acquaintance I hadn't seen in a while. When I told her I was pregnant with twins, she blurted, "Oh no!"

I managed a terse, "Actually, we're very excited."

But the worst part of her reaction—beyond the rudeness of it—was that it reflected, a little bit, the way I felt. Like we'd won some kind of reproductive booby prize.

During the first trimester, I could barely get my head around the fact that I was pregnant at all, let alone with twins. I had plenty of typical pregnancy symptoms: I felt queasy if I went too long without eating, developed an intense loathing for chicken and most dinner foods, and frequently hankered for strange things like Popsicles and Sour Patch Kids. I was tired as all get-out, and usually fell into bed by eight o'clock. A couple of times at work I actually tried (but failed) to snooze in the supply closet—I was so desperately exhausted. And I obviously wasn't showing yet, but I was bloated, for sure, and soon developed what looked sort of like a boozy sorority girl's belly.

Still, the fact that I had two would-be human beings inside my body, just growing and developing away in there, without my doing a blessed thing, was something I had to take on faith. An abstraction. Meanwhile, I was still trying to adjust my vision of myself as mother to my new, dual reality, while at the same time trying not to get *too* adjusted to anything: one or both of these pregnancies could still fail.

It wasn't until the end of the first trimester, when I had to start leaving the top button of my pants unbuttoned and we started telling people besides our family and closest friends that I was pregnant with twins, that it began to feel more real.

In late June, during the eleventh week of my pregnancy, I went to a writer's colony in Vermont for a two-week writing retreat. I figured I'd better get a helluva lot of writing done before these babies came along if I wanted to finish my novel before they were in kindergarten. The other residents fell into two basic groups: unmarried, childless twenty-somethings and married or divorced fiftyish women. There was only one other woman in her thirties—and she had a three-year-old back at home.

I told people I was pregnant with twins if it came up. The twenty-somethings seemed fascinated, bewildered, and a little bit frightened by this. But the older women ate it up. They regaled me with tales of their own pregnancies, births, and parenting experiences; gave me advice; and asked me how I was feeling. One day, over oatmeal, an earth-mother type in dangly ceramic earrings asked me, smiling eagerly, "So, do you talk to them?"

Talk to them? Was I supposed to be doing this? Was something wrong with me that I hadn't? That it had never even occurred to me? They weren't even the size of kiwi fruits yet (or was it mangoes?), according to the Baby Center e-mails. Was I already supposed to have a relationship with them?

"Not really," I told her. "Well, in my head, I guess." (Lie.)

"I always talked to my daughters before they were born," she said. "And they talked to me."

She told me how she could "hear" her firstborn, in utero, saying, *Here I am! Here I am!*

"But my second born," she said, tucking her chin and putting on a wry smile, "said, 'Here I come! Here I come!' And that's exactly what she was like as a child and what she's like as an adult. Look out world, here I come."

That night, as I was lying in bed in my room—it wasn't even nine o'clock; the twenty-somethings were just gearing up, and I could hear them laughing and talking on a porch somewhere—I put my hand on my abdomen and gave it a try. "So, little Sea Monkeys," I said (my pet name of choice for the proto-babies I didn't talk to), "how are you doing in there? I'm trying to take good care of you and keep you healthy. And, um, I'm really looking forward to meeting you."

I listened. They didn't say anything. And I felt like an idiot.

This just wasn't me. I would talk to them when I felt like talking to them. For now, I just wanted to carry them around and keep them safe and let them do their thing while I continued to adjust to the fact that they existed at all—and prepared myself for their arrival into the world.

But just a few days after I returned home from Vermont, as I was walking back to work after lunch, I felt an odd little twinge in the right side of my abdomen. And even though it was much too early to feel any fetal movement, and even though I knew that what I'd felt was most likely my black bean burrito being digested (I was doing my best to abstain from olive loaf *and* turkey), I touched my belly and said quietly, "Hey, little monkey on the right, you OK in there? You dancing? Or is your brother/sister pushing you around?"

A week or so later, I had my thirteen-week ultrasound for prenatal testing, and was utterly relieved to see that there were, in fact, two little babies in there: two tiny, wiggly little skeletons with feet and arms and fingers and toes, kicking and swimming and sucking their thumbs.

"Two babies," I said to Alastair as we walked outside together afterward.

"Two babies," he said.

Feeling like a kindergartner with a crush, I added, "I think I love them."

Shortly after that ultrasound, I signed up to be a member of my local MOT club. That stands for Mothers of Twins, and if you're expecting twins yourself, I recommend hooking up with one of these organizations for the moral support, not to mention the used clothing and equipment, of other women in the same boat. The fact that these organizations are slanted toward mothers of twins, as opposed to just parents of twins, has always bothered Alastair and me. But dads do show up at MOT club events and on the message boards.

However, you might want to wait until *after* you have said twins to join up.

Once a month, my MOT club has what are called COPE meetings. COPE is an acronym for something, I think, but the word itself says it all: come to the meeting, meet other mothers of twins, and help each other cope with the challenges of twin mothering. Soon after I became a member of the club, I decided to go to one of these meetings for a preview of what I was in for.

In retrospect, this was a mistake.

Before I even got inside the house where the meeting was

being held, I felt out of my depth, parking my battered, ten-year-old, bumper-sticker-emblazoned Honda Civic among the new-model minivans and SUVs lined up outside, each of them equipped with two car seats.

This, I thought sinkingly, *is my future.* But there was no way we could afford a minivan or SUV on our semi-employed artist salaries. Not to mention that I didn't *want* to have to drive a minivan or SUV. (The earth! The earth!) But the fact that Alastair needed to push the driver's seat of our small Japanese car back practically to the trunk in order to get his big old American legs inside did not bode well for fitting two infant seats in the back.

Once the meeting got started, I felt better. The women I met were perfectly nice and down-to-earth and congratulatory. "You're going to do just fine," they assured me over tea and cookies (of which I ate approximately twelve). "It's hard, but it's completely worth it."

But soon enough the war stories began. Tales of going forty-eight hours without sleep. Cracked nipples and thrush. Pairs of colicky babies who took turns screaming for three hours straight. Not to mention the complications of pregnancy and birth: gestational diabetes, preeclampsia, bed rest, babies born prematurely and spending harrowing weeks in the ICU.

"But congratulations," they told me, smiling fondly as I left. "It's worth it, really."

"We're dead," I told Alastair when I got home, flopping down onto the couch.

He listened patiently to my account of the evening, then said, "I don't think you should go to any more of those meetings."

I told him that I heartily agreed.

"And," he added, "you should stop reading all those books."

I'd started reading a few "practical tips for raising twins" type books, which made taking care of twins sound like one of those god-awful word problems I used to dread in math class: if baby A nurses for twenty-five minutes starting at 8:30 A.M. on the right breast and baby B nurses for seventeen minutes starting at 9:04 A.M. on the left breast, and both babies need to eat every one and a half to three hours, when should you plan on feeding baby A again, and on which breast?

"We'll be OK," Alastair said. "It's going to be hard, but we'll do it. People have twins. They survive."

Alastair is a very rational person. One of the many lovely things he brings to our marriage is the ability to help me keep things in perspective. Not that it always works.

"I think we should start looking on Craigslist for an SUV," I said. "Or a bigger car. Or maybe my parents will sell us their old Subaru Forester, cheap. They've been talking about getting a new car and maybe—"

"Yeah, maybe. But, listen, we've got another six months to figure all that out, baby. So calm down and shut up and I'll go get you a Popsicle and let's watch *Lost*."

Almost every woman who's ever been pregnant has a story about somebody touching her belly uninvited. But belly touching isn't the only invasion of personal space that happens when you're in that most delicate of conditions. When you're pregnant, it's as if suddenly the whole world is a small, insular village—the kind with a well in the square and a council of elders and chickens running everywhere—and everyone feels they are entitled to make folksy chitchat about your body, your family, your sex life, etc.

This is doubly the case (as are so many things) when you're

having twins. The number one question I was asked while pregnant was, hands down, "do twins run in your family?" It sounds innocent enough, and maybe I'm being paranoid here, but I always got the feeling that people who asked it were probing to see whether or not I'd had fertility treatments. Especially when their follow-up question (after I replied "no" or, more likely, "now they do!") was "so, were you surprised?" To me, it sounded like what they were really asking was "were you surprised, or did you know that this was a possibility since you had BIG FAT FERTILITY TREATMENTS??"

It's not that I was ashamed of the fact that we'd had "help" getting pregnant. I just felt like it wasn't anyone's freakin' business. Fertility treatments involve having fluids drawn and hormone levels tested, getting your private parts poked and prodded, and, if you're a man, getting amorous with a paper cup. It's a very personal decision, about a highly personal matter. I was happy to discuss it with my good friends or disclose it as I saw fit. But it irked me to no end when people asked.

Of course, the indirect questions weren't nearly as bad as some of the more direct ones, like the insulting "Are they natural?" (*No, they're a Rayon-Lycra blend*) and the mind-boggling "Was it on purpose?" (*Yep, we just used the twins position, and voila!*)

The questions didn't stop once the girls were born, either. People still regularly ask me if twins run in my family. But at this point I'm so over it that I'm much more likely to call their bluff and say, "Nope. Fertility drugs."

There were some pregnancy questions, on the other hand, that I loved. Like, "Can you tell who's who when they're moving around?" Because this was one of the coolest parts of being pregnant with two: I really did feel like there were two separate babies inside of me. I wasn't always entirely sure who was moving, or what part of their body I was feeling, but I could generally sense that the baby up top, Baby B, did a whole lot of kicking and punching, while Baby A, down below, tended to be more subdued. This might have been in part because her sister was squishing her, but we nevertheless ascribed to her a calmer demeanor. The baby up top, we decided, must be something of a spitfire. Turns out they're both spitfires. So we were half-right, anyway.

It was right around the time I began to feel the babies move that I started getting genuinely excited about all the things that might turn out to be great about having twins: marveling at the differences and similarities between them, watching them interact with each other, holding them both close to me at once.

Almost all the mothers of twins I talked to while I was pregnant assured me that while twins meant double the work, they also meant double the joy. It sounded an awful lot like propaganda to me at the time. I didn't—and still don't—think it's possible to measure things like joy or love or happiness. Is a person with one child half as happy as someone with two? If I had ten children, would I be ten times as happy?

But I do understand now that having twins comes with a singular (ha) *kind* of joy. You have not just one smiling face to get all googly-eyed at, but two. Two pairs of feet to nibble on. Two tiny butts to lower into the tub. Two different-feeling but equally satisfying bundles of baby to hold in your arms. Two gloriously unique beings that you love equally but in completely different ways.

My friend who had twins a couple of years before I did, who patiently reassured me throughout my pregnancy whenever I started to panic, described it to me as "a funny sort of abundance."

I couldn't have said it better.

3

Alastair and I had had our first conversation about names back when he came up to visit me during my writing residency in Vermont. We had vowed not to broach the subject until we were out of the first-trimester woods, which we weren't quite at that point. But we couldn't help ourselves.

We were in the midst of a day hike in the Long Trail State Forest, taking a break by the edge of a small mountain pond, when Alastair said, "So, how do you feel about Moses?"

"Moses the biblical figure?" I asked.

"Moses as a name for a boy."

I hoped he was kidding, but suspected he wasn't. "Um, no."

"Come on, Moses Moock? How badass a name is that?" (I didn't take Alastair's last name when we got married, but we had decided that our children would have it.)

"He'd have to be a musician to pull it off," I said.

"Exactly."

I rolled my eyes. "If we want to end up in a good nursing

home, we should probably give these babies lawyer or doctor names. And anyway. *Moses?*"

"You can name the other one," he said. "Aren't you glad we're having twins?"

We spent the rest of our hike tossing names back and forth, and quickly realized that naming twins was a complicated matter. We didn't want "coordinating" names (e.g., Molly and Millie, Brendan and Brandon, Jim and Tim), but we also knew that the two names would often be said in the same breath, so they couldn't completely clash (e.g., Isadora and . . . Bob. Moses and . . . anything).

For some reason, I was convinced that I was having two boys. I don't know where this hunch came from, but I was so certain that I even managed to convince the skeptical Alastair. And by the time I had the big sex-revealing, twenty-week ultrasound a few weeks later, we had generated a long list of potential boy names. We only had one girl name picked out, and it was something horrible, like Prunella or Dolores.

So we were once again thrown for a loop when we discovered that we were, in fact, having "two little girls" as the ultrasound tech sweetly put it.

Alastair was thrilled. He'd been hoping my hunch was wrong. With girls, he explained, there would be less pressure on him. He wouldn't have to teach our children "how to be men" (his words) or how to fight ("or not fight"—my words). Best of all, he wouldn't have to have the dreaded sex talk with them. Not that he thought having girls was going to be all tea parties and getting his hair braided. But he felt that somehow he'd have a bit more leeway.

I'd felt the same way about having boys: there wouldn't be as much pressure on me to be a role model or confidante. I could just be my boys' adored mama, who they think is the most beautiful and perfect woman in the world. I guess you could say I liked the idea of creating a little man or two to worship and love me unconditionally. (Is that wrong?)

Girls seemed a lot more complicated, and therefore scary. What if I disappointed them, messed them up, or scarred them emotionally? What if they ended up hating me for their entire adolescence and beyond?

Growing up, I never "hated" my mother. But I was—like a typical teenage girl, I suppose—much more critical of her than I was of my father. And it must have hurt her. Still, on the whole, our relationship had always been good. Especially as I matured into adulthood. As I tried to adjust to the fact that there weren't any penises in my uterus—no baby Moses in my rushes—I reminded myself of this.

I also told myself that, if nothing else, I could probably be a good role model for my daughters. I'd done pretty well for myself, after all: Studied hard. Traveled the world. Had healthy relationships with men, notably my husband. Pursued my career dreams and would (I hoped) continue to do so while also being a mother. I was a basically nice person, too.

And although it frightened me a bit—because intimacy is always a double-edged sword—I warmed up to the special kind of closeness I might have with my girls: the things they might confide in me and the conversations we might have about friendship and love and heartbreak.

Not to mention the fun stuff—the potential "female bonding" activities, which I began to get a taste of even in pregnancy. When I went to prenatal yoga classes, I'd say to Alastair, "the girls and I are going to yoga class, and then we're going to get smoothies." Which was sorta fun. Not that you can't go to yoga and get smoothies with your sons. But it's probably less likely.

And sometimes at those yoga classes, especially toward the end of my pregnancy, when labor was more imminent and downward dog was more like prostrate yak, while lying on my side in a modified shavasana pose at the end of the practice, I'd curl my arm over my belly and have talks with my girls about what was to come (My earth-mother pal from Vermont would have been so proud!): *I can't wait to meet you two and I promise to be the best mother I can be. But I hope you'll forgive me when I screw up, which I inevitably sometimes will.* Or: *This whole giving birth thing—we're going to get through it together, the three of us, as a team, right? We're going to be just fine, right?*

About six months into my pregnancy—before I became so ginormous that I could barely fit into that small Japanese car of ours—Alastair and I went to The Baby Superstore That Shall Not Be Named to register for the necessary baby supplies. There were two baby showers for us being held in the near future (a bit early to account for the risk of my going into labor preterm), so it was time to get down to business.

If I had it to do over again, I would have solicited advice from all my parent friends as well as the Mothers of Twins Club; researched larger items, like car seats and strollers, online ahead of time; and gone to the store with detailed notes, a checklist, and probably a snack.

What we actually did was go more or less unprepared, with a few things jotted down on a scrap of notebook paper. The woman at the registry desk gave us a thick, stapled packet of "recommended items," many of which seemed entirely unnecessary (a baby wipe warmer? really?).

"You don't have a list specifically for people having twins, do you?" I asked. There were enough of us around that it didn't seem entirely unlikely.

"Well, no, I'm afraid we don't," the woman said. Then added, cheerily, "I guess just get twice as much of everything!"

"Right!" I said. Even though I knew she wasn't.

Obviously, there were some things we'd need to double up on: car seats, crib bedding, etc. But we didn't need two diaper bags or baby bathtubs or breast pumps. And there were other items I suspected we could probably get away with 1.5 times as many of, like washcloths, towels, bottles, and bibs.

Still, after wandering aimlessly around the store for about ten minutes, I felt utterly paralyzed and vaguely queasy. Even the calm and rational Alastair was visibly flustered, overwhelmed by the sheer volume of stuff: six different kinds of baby bathtubs. Twelve different kinds of bottles. Ten thousand different kinds of car seats, strollers, blankets, portacribs, and sheets. Plus things we didn't even know existed before we entered the store, like sleep positioners and pacifier clips and the aforementioned wipe warmer.

We were stymied by the choices, and the twin factor multiplied our confusion. The nurse at the multiples class we'd gone to at the hospital—which, like so many things designed to educate and prepare future parents of twins only served to terrify us further—told us we should buy at least twenty bottles. *Twenty.* She reasoned that we'd go through them fast and wouldn't want to be constantly washing them between feedings. This seemed to make sense. On the other hand, I was planning to breast-feed, so maybe we didn't need that many. Or did we? Maybe I'd be able to pump so much milk that I'd be filling up bottles left and right. On the other *other* hand, maybe I wouldn't be able to handle nursing two babies, and we'd end up switching to formula anyway. And by twenty bottles, did she mean six-ounce ones? Eight-ounce? Twelve-ounce? (Would our babies ever, at any point, be drinking twelve ounces of milk or formula at once?)

I think I stood in front of the bottle section with the damned scanner gun in my hand for twenty minutes, frozen, staring into middle space. Alastair had to practically whack me on the back of the head to get me moving again.

"You know," he reminded me, "we can always get more. Or return them if we get too many."

This was absolutely, 100 percent true. My slow-mo brain could manage to acknowledge that much. I also knew that women had been successfully raising children—including twins—for millennia without baby superstores or registry lists or ergonomically correct baby bottles. I knew that a baby could sleep in the proverbial dresser drawer. And yet I still felt like I was about to cry.

We ended up with all the essential baby gear we needed and more, of course. Between baby showers and hand-me-downs and many—many—trips back and forth to The Baby Superstore That Shall Not Be Named in the first weeks and months of our girls' lives, we were well beyond well-equipped. And sure, maybe we bought a few more bottles than we needed, and maybe we were a little short on burp cloths sometimes. But, amazingly, we all survived.

I was fortunate that I didn't have to go on bed rest at any point in my pregnancy, and could more or less go about my routine as usual. Toward the end of my second trimester, though, I had to give up my daily fifteen-minute walk from our house to the T station when I found myself feeling dizzy and faint along the way. I started driving to the station instead, and that was going just fine. But then, one Monday morning as I sat on the crowded train, reading *Middlemarch,* I started feeling dizzy again. I put my book away, leaned over, and put my elbows on my knees. Closed my eyes. Breathed in and out. And then . . .

Next thing I knew, I was lying across the seat next to mine, and a young woman was crouching in front of me, touching my shoulder, and asking me if I was all right. There was vomit on the seat, and in my hair. The train was stopped, and, as I sat up, a train official of some sort came on board and asked me if I needed an ambulance.

An ambulance? I thought groggily. *How would they get an ambulance onto a train?*

Meanwhile, a couple of women on the train were handing me tissues and napkins, to wipe the puke—which, by that time, I'd ascertained was my own—out of my hair.

As it turns out, the station we were stopped at was right near the hospital where I planned to deliver. So all the T official had to do was walk me across the street to my obstetrician, who checked the babies' heartbeats and my vital signs. Everything was fine, but I was told that I should (1) Eat more protein in the mornings and (2) Stop taking the train, if possible.

So I started driving to work instead. But this required parking in a garage and walking another five minutes from there to the office. One morning around my thirty-second week of pregnancy, as I was making the walk—waddle would be more accurate—I felt a sudden, sharp, shooting pain deep inside my body, as if someone was sticking a needle up through my cervix.

(Who knew you could feel things in your cervix?) I froze where I was and waited for it to pass.

A young man coming toward me from the opposite direction saw this happen, and he froze, too, a look of sheer panic on his face.

"Are you OK?" he asked, in a way that made it clear he really, *really* hoped that I was.

I told him, calmly, smiling, that I was just fine. Thank you.

"You're sure?" (Translation: Please don't go into labor right now, thus making me morally obligated to assist you.)

"I'm sure," I said. "Thank you."

I started working from home not long after that.

And at just shy of thirty-five weeks, at which point it had become difficult to sit at a desk and simultaneously reach the keyboard, I stopped working altogether.

I was big. Damned big. And I was totally over being pregnant. I had exactly two maternity tops that fit me and my pelvis felt like it was about to crack in two. I couldn't get comfortable in bed, even with all manner of pregnancy pillows, folded blankets, and other props, and I had excruciating heartburn every night around 1:00 A.M., regardless of what or how little I'd eaten hours earlier at dinner. Plus, I had a persistent and sometimes stabbing pain beneath my right rib (somebody's foot?) and another in the middle left side of my back (somebody else's elbow?)—oh yes, and middle-of-the night charley horses. We mustn't forget the charley horses.

I was also antsy as all get-out. Nobody had ever told me how tedious the last weeks of pregnancy would be. I'd spent months getting used to and excited about the idea of these babies. I'd set up the nursery and prewashed the sheets and teeny-tiny PJs in fragrance-free detergent. I'd read the baby-care books. But I'd come to realize that, no matter how much I prepared, nothing could fully prepare me for what was about to happen. I was going to have to learn on the job. And I wanted to get started, please.

Which is why on the day that marked thirty-six weeks— considered full term for twins—I started taking measures to get things moving. I enlisted all of the folk remedies for labor induction: warm baths, brisk walks (as brisk as was possible for someone of my girth), raspberry-leaf tea, and spicy foods. Even sex, though it was about the last thing I felt like doing. Having to wear sweatpants and shlubby, extra-large maternity sweaters, being constantly achy, and feeling exhausted all the time doesn't exactly get one's libido fired up. Or one's husband's.

But none of it seemed to do a thing. Not even a single Braxton-Hicks contraction to give me hope. And when I went to my OB appointment a few days later, my doctor declared me only a smidgeon dilated. It was beginning to feel like these babies had resolved to stay inside me as long as was fetally possible.

Alastair and I spent a quiet Christmas at home, just the two of us, with a grocery store rotisserie chicken and an apple pie, waiting. And waiting. We did make it out for a Christmas Eve service at our local Unitarian Universalist church, and I swear every head in every pew turned toward me when they read the part about Mary being "great with child." I was great, all right.

By the next day, we were practically tearing our hair out with boredom. We took a walk around Harvard Square, got Indian food (extra spicy!), and spent the evening in front of the TV. In the course of the day I had two, maybe three, very mild cramps. But nothing that suggested the start of labor.

Then, around 11:30, as I was heaving myself into bed, I felt a little "pop!" followed by a warm, wet, spreading sensation.

You have never seen a gigantic pregnant woman jump out of bed and run to the bathroom so fast. We'd changed the sheets *that very morning.* So, seriously: forget spicy food, raspberry-leaf tea, and sex. If you want your water to break, change the sheets and get into bed.

Sitting on the toilet, I called to Alastair, still downstairs. "Hey baby? Um . . . my water just broke."

A pause. "Are you sure?"

I looked down at my pajama bottoms and underwear, in a drenched heap on the bathroom floor. "Yeah, pretty sure."

More than 50 percent of twin births are done via C-section. But my girls were both head-down, in ideal position for a traditional (I hate the word "vaginal") birth, and I was determined to deliver them that way. I'm not a squeamish person in general, but I found the idea of someone cutting through my skin and muscles rather unsavory. I also wasn't keen on the whole epidural thing, having had a really, really painful experience with a botched spinal tap a few years earlier. Plus, overachiever that I am, I wanted to get through the birth without drugs if I could.

But from the minute we arrived at the hospital, shortly before 1:00 A.M., it seemed that every doctor, nurse, and anesthesiologist was assuming that as a twin mother, I'd go under the knife and, in the meantime, drug myself to the hilt.

The on-call obstetrician—an awkward, skittish little man who must have been out sick the day in medical school they taught bedside manner—admitted that he'd never actually delivered twins in the traditional manner, only via C-section. And he didn't do breech extractions, so if I managed to give birth to the first baby (OK, OK) vaginally and then the second baby turned feet first, we'd have to go to C-section for her.

He then informed me that I could get my epidural whenever I wanted. "It's pretty much standard procedure for twins," he said.

I informed him that, actually, it was my decision. (Meanwhile, I should note, my contractions, which had started almost immediately after my water broke, were becoming stronger and more frequent. So I really wasn't in the mood to be going tête-à-tête with the medical industry.)

The doctor then informed me, rather condescendingly, that I'd most likely need a C-section, and if I didn't have an epidural, they'd have to use general anesthesia. "And you don't want that, do you?"

At which point Alastair asked him when his shift ended.

That shut him up. But I was already feeling defeated and dispirited. All I wanted—just like any other mother about to be—was to have some sense of control over how my labor and birth were going to go. Was that entirely off the table for me just because I happened to be having two babies at once? Did I not even have the right to hope for a routine, possibly even drug-free birth? For the rest of my life, I was going to be a mother of twins—an experience completely different from that of 97 percent of other mothers in the world. Couldn't I just have this one last normal thing?

At least, I thought, the labor nurses would be on my side. They'd be supportive, help me manage the pain, and coach me through the contractions. Just like in the videos we'd watched in our birthing class (the same birthing class where—sigh—the instructor kept stopping to look at us and say, "this actually doesn't apply to you, since you're having twins . . .").

But the nurse on call, though friendly enough, wasn't actually that helpful. My contractions were coming fast, hard, and furious by the time we got into the labor and delivery room, but the nurse didn't have much in the way of encouragement or advice to offer. Just "try to relax as much as you can." She was more focused (and I suppose I can't fault her for this) on getting the fetal monitors strapped onto my belly and getting a trace on the girls' heartbeats, which wasn't easy to do. I had to lie on the bed as still as possible while this was happening—which is not easy when you feel like someone has affixed a large vise to your lower back and abdomen and is steadily, mercilessly tightening it.

I was getting scared. I knew labor was going to hurt, but I hadn't realized just how much. When my mother told me about her (drug-free) labor with my brother and me, she described it as feeling like "extra-strong menstrual cramps." She remembered it as being not so much painful as "hard work." I had hoped that, through the power of genetics, it would be the same for me.

Maybe my mother has a higher pain tolerance. Or amnesia. Either way, I clearly wasn't having the kind of labor she recalled. Then again, she only gave birth to one baby at a time. And yet I still felt like maybe I just wasn't managing the pain the right way. Or maybe I just wasn't strong enough.

For the next hour or so, Alastair valiantly rubbed my back and shoulders, fed me ice chips, endured my cursing, and even managed to make me laugh a few times. He also periodically helped disentangle me from the tubing of the contraction and fetal-heart-rate monitors and pulled the damned hospital johnny back up onto my shoulders when it slipped off. Prelabor, I'd had visions of managing the pain by assuming wolf-woman primitive squatting poses and channeling lunar energy and whatnot, but on account of all the crap hooked onto me, this proved impossible.

I began to understand why the people in the earthy-crunchy natural childbirth books I'd read were all naked. I would have killed to be naked.

It was right after I puked that Alastair gently suggested that maybe I should get the epidural. "We can do whatever you want," he said. "But it could be a few more hours of this, and I just worry that when you get to the pushing part, you'll be totally exhausted." At the most recent cervical check, I'd only been three and a half centimeters dilated. But my contractions were already only a few seconds apart, and the pain was constant and knife-sharp in my lower back.

Feeling another wave of nausea coming on, I agreed, secretly relieved, that he was probably right.

The epidural was fucking amazing. Suddenly, the contractions felt like gentle cramps, nothing more. I felt infinitely less anxious. I even got an hour or so of sleep. I woke up praising modern technology, the medical establishment, and the merciful (and not bad-looking) anesthesiologist who had so gently and expertly administered the blessed spinal drip.

And then, somewhere around 7:30 A.M., I started feeling an undeniable urge to push. When the doctor came in—a different one now, a very competent-seeming young woman, thank God—I asked if there was anything I should be doing to resist this urge. She thrust her arm elbow-deep into me and reported that I was fully dilated. Push away.

Now I was excited: we were on the homestretch. We were gonna get these babies *born*!

This part of the process was actually quite satisfying. And surprisingly comical: I had to assume all manner of absurd contortions—lying on my side, getting on all fours, semi-squatting and holding on to a bar over the bed—while gritting my teeth and straining every muscle in my body and making, I'm sure, completely ridiculous noises. And the doctor kept saying, "Push into your rectum! All right there in your rectum! Like you're making a bowel movement!"

While all this was going on, what seemed like the entire maternity ward medical staff was parading in and out of the room, introducing themselves, some of them even extending a hand for me to shake:

"Hi! We're Babs and Carol, the pediatric nurses who'll be at the birth!"

"Hey there, I'm Fred, the pediatrician for Baby A, and this is Barney, the pediatrician for Baby B!"

"Greetings! I'm Ollie the anesthesiologist, and this is my assistant, Stanley!"

"Like, hi, nice to meet you, we're Madison and Addison, the first-year medical students who'll be watching this whole random thing, right?"

"Hello! I'm Jim, the orderly who will be mopping the blood and amniotic fluid up off the floor after you give birth!"

We'd been warned ahead of time that because I was having twins there would be a staff the size of a softball team at the delivery, but after the fifth or sixth person came in to say hidey-ho and make chitchat, I looked over at Alastair and we gave each other looks like, "Dude, what's with the welcome wagon? We're trying to give birth here!"

Meanwhile, the OB was still urging me to push everything into my rectum, and I could have sworn her thumb was up my butt. Given that I was about to pass two children through my vagina, the whole thing was surprisingly ass-focused.

Then, things got dicey. And my anxiety took an uptick again: Baby A's umbilical cord was wrapped around her neck, causing her heartbeat to dip with each push, and she wasn't making any downward progress. All the hard work I was doing wasn't actually accomplishing anything.

The doctor told us she'd try some suction, and if that didn't work we'd have to go to C-section. But hearing the dreaded C-word, I summoned all of my primal, wolf-woman, moon-goddess strength. I sent silent messages to my baby: *Come on. You can do this. We can do this.* I gave a few colossal pushes (into my rectum) and did it: I got things moving. I was so proud of myself—and of my little girl.

In fact, I still tell her the story today: how she was having trouble, and things weren't looking good, but we did it. Together, we did it.

Now, I was wheeled into the operating room (which really *is* standard procedure for twin births, in case an emergency C-section is needed) for the grand finale.

More pushing, some Pitocin when I was bleeding a bit too much, a small episiotomy, which I didn't even feel, and lots of excited shouting from Alastair and the docs alike: *We can see the head! You're almost there! One more big push! Here she comes!*

And finally, at 9:28 A.M., Baby A was born. She was held up for me to see, but whisked quickly away to transitional care for oxygen and monitoring, as the length and difficulty of her birth had left her a bit worse for the wear. Meanwhile, the doctors were prodding my belly to get Baby B into position. I braced myself for another long round of pushing, but the child practically popped out like a cork. She had a good healthy cry and seemed royally peeved to have been evicted from her comfortable penthouse in the womb. Time of birth: 9:37 A.M.

. . .

What seemed like minutes later, we were back in our labor room, babes in our arms, looking out the window at a panoramic view of the Charles River, feeling at once exhausted and exhilarated.

In the previous few weeks, we had finalized our decision on names. For Baby A, we had settled on Elsa. The slightly old-fashioned, elegant sound of Elsa—inspired by Ingrid Bergman's character in *Casablanca*—seemed like it would be right for her, quiet and patient as we imagined her to be, sleeping under her sister in the womb. It took us a long time to decide on the second name, but ultimately we chose Clio—the name of the Greek muse of history and epic poetry, who was sometimes referred to as the Proclaimer. This seemed to suit Baby B's spunky in utero kicking and punching.

But now, as we sat side by side on the bed, each of us holding one of the girls, we wondered: had we chosen the right names? Moreover, had we chosen the right name for the right baby?

"Are you Clio?" I asked, looking down at Baby B's round, sleeping face: She had her father's upturned nose, broad mouth, and wide-set eyes.

"Is she?" Alastair asked, as if she had answered, and he just hadn't heard.

"I think so," I said. "And"—I looked at the baby in his arms—"she looks like an Elsa to me."

She was delicate and almost elfin, with a pointed chin, cupid's-bow mouth, and almond-shaped eyes—like mine. (She had my blood type, too, while Clio had Alastair's—conclusive proof that they were, in fact, fraternal, as we had assumed all along; almost all twins that result from fertility treatments are.)

"Yeah, I guess she is an Elsa," Alastair said. "God, it's hard to believe they're going to become *people*."

"And hard to believe they're our *children*."

For thirty-seven weeks, we'd readied ourselves for their arrival, and I must have thought, on some level, that when they were born, they would feel instantly familiar.

Instead, they felt like two little strangers—beautiful and fragile and barely there. We didn't know them at all, except to know that they had just transformed us completely. Whether or not we felt like it yet, we were parents now—an instant family of four.

"Look," I said, and nodded toward the window. It had started snowing.

4

Ever read **A Prayer for Owen Meany** by John Irving? The title character, Owen Meany, is an incredibly short boy with a strange, high-pitched voice and a host of quirky interests and abilities, among them speaking Vietnamese and holding his breath for long periods of time. Just after the climax of the novel, the narrator of the book realizes that Owen's unique characteristics were what enabled him to perform a final, heroic feat—as if his whole life had been leading up to that one moment.

This is sort of, just a tiny bit, how I felt after giving birth to Elsa and Clio.

There are a lot of things I am not good at, among them arithmetic, team sports, stand-up comedy, and going easy on myself. But there are a few things I have always done well: I'm a good planner and organizer. I'm detail-oriented and have the ability to think several steps ahead. I am an excellent multitasker, exhibit strong leadership abilities, and perform well under pressure. (And yes, I am quite good at job interviews.)

So, whereas I'd initially thought I was totally *not* suited to parenting twins, I had the sense, in the first hours and days after the girls were born, that maybe I was, in fact, ideally suited.

Even in the hospital, still groggy and achy from labor, I was making lists and giving orders: Mom, you need to go to The Baby Superstore That Shall Not Be Named and pick up a changing pad and a couple of covers, plus a few packs of preemie-sized sleepers. (At just shy of five pounds, the girls were swimming in their newborn-sized clothes). Dad, go to this obscure pharmacy in Cambridge, whose address I've written here, along with a small map, to rent the hospital-grade breast pump the lactation consultant wrote down here, which our insurance will pay for. Alastair, as soon as we get home, you need to set up the Pack 'N Play and we'll keep it in the living room as a downstairs sleeping place. And do we have cat food? I think we're out of cat food.

There were, admittedly, times during the first few days that I got a bit kooky and control freaky as CEO of Operation Twins. At one point, for example, I started fretting about our lack of surfaces to put things on. There was just so much *stuff* that was a part of the feeding routine during the first week. Because the girls were so small, we had to supplement my not-quite-there-yet breast milk with formula, which we administered via little feeding tubes and catheters that we held up to my breasts so the girls could practice sucking on them (my breasts, that is) while also getting the formula. I also, to my chagrin and annoyance, had to use nipple shields—floppy, clear plastic things with fembot-sized fake nipples—until the girls got better at latching on. Then there were the storage bottles for pumped milk. A big glass of water for me, always. Plus nipple cream, nursing pads, and other supplies and implements I can't currently recall. Tissues, maybe? The TV remote? A can opener?

In any case, I just didn't feel like we had enough places to put all this crap, and I was stressed out about trying to make the whole damned twin breast-feeding thing work, so I ordered Alastair to go out and buy TV tray tables. Like, immediately. He expressed his confusion as to why, exactly, we needed them.

"Just go buy them," I said. "Now."

The next day I found myself sitting on the couch with a baby or two in my arms, looking quizzically at one of our two new really ugly, white, utilitarian, "As Seen on TV" tray tables, asking Alastair, "Why, exactly, did I think we needed these?"

We returned them to the store two days later. And we still laugh about them today.

In addition to being patient with my occasional bouts of irrationality, Alastair is highly organized himself. He was right there with me when it came to cataloging who sent us what gifts, for thank-you note purposes. (We were astounded and humbled by the number of gifts and bouquets we were sent in the weeks after the girls were born, from friends and family around the globe.)

And he was conscientious about documenting feedings and diaper changes, as we'd been instructed at the hospital to do. We kept a spiral notebook where we noted what time and how long each feeding for each baby lasted, and on what breast, and how much formula or breast milk they downed from bottles, if applicable. We also noted diaper contents: Lots of poop. A little poop. Major pee. Maybe some pee? Spit up, no spit up. We still have this notebook, actually, and looking at it now, it's like some crazy Mayan code. I have no idea what any of it means.

But I do remember the anxious meticulousness with which we kept it. The girls, skinny-limbed and floppy-necked, seemed so small, so fragile, so barely ours. By recording their every biological intake and expulsion, I felt as if we were keeping them tethered more tightly to life.

We might have gone a little overboard in our type A approach to the first weeks of the girls' lives. Eventually, of course, we dispensed with the notebook and stopped analyzing diaper contents. We trusted our instincts more. But I think our early organization machinations served an important purpose: they gave us a sense, however illusory, of control in what was a completely new and utterly overwhelming situation.

We couldn't control when our babies slept or why they cried or how much they ate. We couldn't even quite grasp the fact that they were *ours* yet. But we could make lists and take notes and buy unnecessary tray tables. That much, we could do.

Breast-feeding made up a major chunk of how I spent my time in the first weeks of the girls' lives. In fact, I'm surprised there isn't still an indentation in our couch, given the hours each day my butt was planted on it. Each baby took from thirty to forty-five minutes to nurse at first, and, after one was finished, I had to move right on to the next. The goal was always to keep them on the same feeding schedule, to the extent that we could. This meant that I had roughly an hour and a half between feedings, during which time I would pump milk so Alastair could do the occasional feeding by bottle.

They say that your body will make as much milk as you need, as long as the demand is there, and, man oh man, did my body make. As a result, 80 percent of the weight I'd gained during pregnancy—all forty-seven pounds of it—was gone before the girls were a month old. This despite the fact that I ate pretty much anything I could get my mouth on.

And I had the awesomest knockers. They really were perfection: generous C-plus cups, the likes of which I'd never had before and never will again, perfectly round and firm. And they were virtual fonts of breast milk.

Still, nursing was frustrating and awkward at first. The girls, being tiny and sleepy and not really experienced at this whole sucking-on-a-boob thing, had trouble latching on. I had to wear the nipple shields, which were forever falling off. And I was never sure how much, if any, milk the girls were getting.

But I was determined to keep at it, in the hope that it would get easier—in part because nursing was one of the few opportunities I had for real one-on-one time with each of the girls. It was also my first opportunity to experience them as distinct individuals, not just small, sleeping (or screaming), almost interchangeable bundles.

The differences between the girls were never as marked as they were when they were on the boob. When Clio nursed, she would get an impish little proto-smile on her Kewpie-doll face—turned-up nose, big eyes—and then her eyelids would sag, and she'd look like a little baby stoner. A minute later, she'd be sound asleep. When she pulled away from—well, fell off—my breast, she'd pout adorably, her lower lip thrust out, her eyebrows lifted, and her chin covered with milk.

Elsa, on the other hand, would have her mouth wide open like a baby bird's before I could even get my shirt up. She'd chug like a frat boy at first, voracious and alert, then downshift into a steady, business-like sucking. She was a noisy little thing, both during and after feedings, with frequent hiccups and burps, and a proclivity toward spitting up. Sometimes with Linda Blair-esque volume and force.

We latched on (so to speak) to these little bits of personality and distinction with a sort of slaphappy desperation, so eager were we to get to know and understand these little creatures in our midst. What's amazing, though, is how much, in retrospect, the girls' behaviors and mannerisms, even at just days and weeks old, were so completely *them*. We really were seeing our daughters' true natures, even though we didn't know it yet.

I hadn't planned to attempt feeding both of the girls at the same time until they were a little bit older and a little less floppy. But Phyllis told me I should go for it.

Phyllis was a postpartum doula who visited us a few times after the girls were born—a gift from Alastair's parents to give us some support and help us find our parenting legs a bit. She was a sassy older woman, tall and thin and white-haired, a tad intense ("You are an extremely strong woman," she told me at our first meeting, before the girls were born. "I can tell that about you.") but very helpful and direct. The first time she came over, when the girls were just a few days old, she told me there was no reason I couldn't start tandem nursing right away. I was hesitant, but she was insistent.

She started rolling up receiving blankets and arranging cushions to get me into position, then gently laid a baby on either side of me on my double nursing pillow, their feet facing behind me and their heads supported in my hands. This was the double clutch, or "football," hold—one of five or six possible positions for nursing twins, and the one I'd continue to use most often when I tandem nursed.

Next, she helped get the babies latched on, one at a time. And they actually both ate a little bit. It was strange—I couldn't help feeling rather animal-like, having two babies suckling at me in this manner. But it was also quite lovely to have them both in my arms, both contented. I even found myself tearing up a bit.

"Look at you," Phyllis said, beaming. "Just look at what you are doing, Jane! Isn't it amazing!"

Amazing, indeed. Until a piece of hair fell in my face, and I flipped my head back to try to get it out of the way, and Clio got jostled off my boob, taking my nipple shield with her. So shield and baby had to be reapplied to me, with Phyllis's help. While that was happening, Elsa came unlatched. And as I was trying to get her back into position, I got an itch on my nose, which I made the mistake of trying to get at with my shoulder, because I really didn't want to ask Phyllis to scratch my nose, though I'm sure she would have happily complied. And now my grip on Elsa's small head had slipped and needed to be readjusted. Meanwhile, Clio was falling asleep. But I (obviously) didn't have any hands free to employ the usual wake-up-Clio techniques—massaging her hands and feet, stroking her cheeks, or stripping off clothing.

Now I was just amazingly frustrated. It was clear that this technique would only work if I had someone right there to assist me and, in effect, be my hands.

So from then on out, most of the time, I stuck to the one-at-a-time approach. Later, when the girls were bigger and stronger and more adept at nursing, I did nurse them together more of the time, especially if time was of the essence. But even then, I still preferred to nurse them singly. It was simpler, snugglier.

There was something almost magical about nursing the girls together though: to be able to nurture at my full biological capacity, both breasts occupied and both arms full of daughter, was a distinctly goddess-y experience. While I was doing it, I did feel strong. Just like Phyllis said. And I felt powerfully connected to Elsa and Clio—almost as if the three of us were one.

I knew that the first weeks and months would be hard. I knew there would be times when we'd feel helpless and bewildered and perplexed, not to mention really, really tired. But I knew the chances were pretty good that we'd get through it, keep our two tiny beings alive, and live to tell the tale.

There was, however, one potential wrench that I feared might fling itself into the works: given my history, there was a much greater chance of my slipping into postpartum depression. And I worried that the stress and exhaustion of parenting twins made the odds even higher.

I couldn't imagine how I'd cope if I got depressed. To take care of one newborn while hobbled by depression would be one thing. But two? Next to impossible. And to be robbed of my ability to participate fully and consciously in the experience of new motherhood would have been so disappointing, so infuriating. Plus, I might have to increase my med dosage or change to entirely new drugs, which could put the kibosh on breast-feeding.

Which is why one of the first things I'd done after finding out I was pregnant was call my psychiatrist. I hadn't seen him since my attempt to go off meds the previous summer and wanted to touch base, just to make sure we had some kind of plan in place in the event that I developed PPD.

But the bastard had disappeared. His name was no longer on the practice's voice-mail directory, and I couldn't reach an operator or receptionist. I even left messages with the other doctors in the practice—nothing. Through some concerted googling, I managed to track the guy down: he'd left clinical practice for a teaching job. Without, apparently, informing his previous patients. Brilliant!

In the midst of my searching for a new psychiatrist, I learned about a study at Massachusetts General Hospital for pregnant women with a history of depression. If I joined, they'd monitor my moods straight through into the postpartum period. I signed up immediately. Eventually, I also found a new psychiatrist— not bearded—and met with her as well. I had my team in place, and I was ready for anything. *Come on, depression, you big bully,* I thought, *let's see what you got.*

Turns out, depression had nothing. In the weeks and months after my girls were born, to my great and enormous relief, it never showed its ugly, dead-eyed face.

Which isn't to say that my mood didn't do any hormonal dipping and swooping over the first couple of weeks. It dipped and swooped pretty damned good, actually. The first days after the girls were born, I experienced strange, even absurd, surges of emotion and tearfulness—not usually in the form of sadness but in the form of a heartfelt awareness (delusion?) of the poignancy and beauty and tragedy of the human condition. Sometimes it made sense: my tears the first time I nursed both babies at the same time, for example.

But then there was stuff like Gerald Ford. He'd died a few days before the girls were born, and *Sixty Minutes* ran a profile of him that we watched, babes in our arms. My mother was there, too, staying at our house for a few days to help us out (I don't think we would have eaten if she hadn't). I remarked to her at one point, tears in my eyes, that Gerald Ford became president just a few months after I was born, and wasn't it poetic and sad, yet beautiful somehow, that he'd died just before *my* babies were born? And, I remarked to Alastair, wasn't it sad that Ford hadn't been more appreciated in his lifetime and that the only thing our generation really associated with him was Chevy Chase's imitation on *Saturday Night Live*? Because Ford was obviously a good man, with good intentions, even if he had pardoned Nixon.

Alastair remarked that maybe I should go upstairs and get some sleep.

Then there were a few days, about two weeks after the girls were born, when I did feel something closer to actual depression— a bleakness that would descend in the afternoons and last into the evenings, carving a pit in the middle of my chest and blocking my ability to feel pleasure or hope. As night fell, promising no real rest, I'd ask myself, What have we done? Why did I ever want children in the first place? When will this get easier? And when will life feel normal again?

But in the morning, waking at first light to lift the girls up from the co-sleeper next to our bed to nurse them, one by one, then going downstairs for coffee and breakfast and the day ahead, life felt all right again. There was a satisfying purity of purpose in the daily rhythm: Feed, feed. Change, change. Rock, rock. Shush, shush.

And then the blues vanished completely. And I can honestly say that the year that followed was one of the happiest of my life. It was when the girls were just over a year old that my old pal depression came back, with a vengeance. But that's a story for later.

5

One of the baby gifts we received was a small quilted mat about two feet square with a couple of criss-crossing arches over it, hung with various soft toys, some of which played music and rattled. It was black and white and red and featured bold, geometric patterns that were supposed to be visible to younger infants and stimulate their brains.

One early morning when the girls were a few weeks old, I put them on the mat to see what would happen. At this point in their lives they were doing little more than sleeping, eating, crying, and sleeping some more. But maybe, I thought, the power of The Stimulator—our pet name for the contraption—would inspire them to do all kinds of exciting things: Kick their feet. Gurgle. Reach. Break into song. The possibilities were endless.

But things didn't go exactly as I'd hoped. Clio—who was sleepy that morning to begin with—just closed her eyes. Elsa lay there for a little while, her eyes open (*She's looking at the colors and patterns!* I thought. *She's going to be a genius!*), and then started screaming until I picked her up and fed her.

So much for The Stimulator.

In retrospect, I think of those first weeks of the girls' lives as a larval stage. Not just because they themselves were sort of larvae-like: tiny and squirmy, responsive to stimuli of the biological variety (hunger, discomfort, fatigue), but not terribly, you know, *interesting.* But because all of us, our foursome, were cocooned in our little life, undergoing a major transition: from the fourth trimester, as it is sometimes aptly called, to the rest of our life as a family.

We hardly ever left the house. Granted, it was the dead of winter. But the constant round-the-clock feedings and the logistical headache of venturing out kept us close to home. People occasionally visited, and when the girls were still very small and sleepy, we actually had friends over for (very) quick dinners a few times. But for the most part, e-mail was our lifeline to friends and family.

World news trickled in to us through the radio, Internet, and television, all of it seeming absurd in its irrelevance to our incubated existence: The wars in Iraq and Afghanistan. The premature stirrings of the next presidential race. The slipping stock market and fear of recession. I found myself musing, in my hazy, milky, sleep-deprived sort of way: what did all this posturing and politicking and predicting matter in the grand scheme of things when this, what we were doing right here and now, felt so much more essential and human?

Individual wars and politicians, celebrities and criminals would come and go—always had, always would. But the nurturing of new human lives was constant. Around the world at any moment, in millions of homes—from Massachusetts to Paraguay to Palestine to China—newborns were crying, sleeping, and passing gas with gusto in their parents' arms, as they had since the dawn of man. It was humanity in its purest form.

And to me at that time, it felt like all that really mattered.

The days blended together, and whether it was Monday or Thursday or Sunday was irrelevant. Alastair wasn't working, except for the occasional guitar lesson or nighttime gig, so he was there to share parenting duties with me 40/60 (the extra 20 percent on my end representing 10 percent for each breast). He did more of the errands, but we frequently let the world come to us instead. We had our groceries delivered more often than not (SO worth the seven-dollar delivery fee) and got friendly with the delivery guy from the pan-Asian restaurant up the street. He was trying to learn English and would sometimes ask us a grammar or vocabulary question as he handed us our pad thai.

There were times when I was so absorbed in our steady rhythm of eating, sleeping, holding, and comforting babies that I flaked out completely—which was not like me at all. Once, I missed a dentist appointment scheduled months before (which they kindly didn't charge me for once I explained why I was feeling a wee bit dotty). Another time, two of my close friends showed up on my doorstep with flowers and scones for a visit that I'd completely forgotten about. I pretended I was expecting them and hastily put on a pot of coffee.

Such was the cocoon: self-contained, simple in purpose, and quiet, when the girls weren't crying. And inside our little pod of a world, Alastair and I were slowly, gradually learning things about parenting twins that would serve us in the years ahead—maybe for the rest of our lives, in some cases.

We learned, first and foremost, that the techniques that worked for soothing one of the girls wouldn't necessarily work for the other. When Elsa was fussy or upset, it was generally nursing or cuddling that appeased her. Clio, on the other hand, wanted space. If we held her close when she was crying, she'd arch her back and scream all the louder. Sometimes all I could do was put her down and leave her alone, and it always broke my heart a little. Was I doing something terribly wrong? Would she always push me away? Other times, she wanted motion. I would hold her in my arms while I bounced vigorously up and down on a yoga ball. Or I'd walk with her around the house, shifting left and right and up and down, or doing a bouncy little stutter-walk. Eventually, she'd calm down.

We also learned how to make order of chaos. Correction: we learned how to tolerate chaos and not lose our shit in the process. Because as hard as we might try to keep the girls contented and happy—feeding them before their hunger made them simultaneously inconsolable, trying our damnedest to keep them on the same sleeping and eating schedules (well, that was more for our benefit, I suppose), and getting them out of wet or dirty diapers within an acceptable time frame—there was only so much we could do. Inevitably there were times when both of the girls were crying and hungry and wet all at the same time, and just when we thought we had the situation under control, someone would spit up or a bottle of freshly pumped breast milk would get knocked over and the cat would start licking it up off the floor, and I'd find myself yelling at the cat, as if it was *her* fault that now I'd have to get up at 3:00 A.M. to nurse the girls instead of letting Alastair do a bottle feeding. And anyway, why didn't she pitch in around here, huh? Fold some laundry or something?

So, correction of correction: we didn't always succeed in

keeping it together in the midst of chaos. But we learned how to recover: Deep breathing. Humor (always good). Or, if I found myself really on the brink, putting the girls in the Pack 'N Play by the bookshelves and giving myself a little time-out. *Step away from the babies, ma'am. I repeat: step away from the babies.*

Still, as intense as the newborn weeks were—as completely as those two small babies had transformed my days and nights—I still didn't feel like *I* had been transformed yet. I don't suppose I expected to feel like a mother starting on day one, but on day ten or eleven seemed a reasonable enough assumption.

But even as I sat in our living room with one baby on my boob and another in a bouncy seat at my feet, surrounded by baby gear and otherwise thoroughly steeped in evidence that I had, in fact, become a mother, it hadn't quite sunk in yet.

Before I was pregnant, I used to have dreams that I had a baby, and then forgot about, or simply ignored him or her. I'd leave the baby with friends or relatives or *somewhere* (it was never quite clear, this being a dream), take off, and go about my business, and then later have the panicked realization that, holy crap, I'd had a baby, and I wasn't even paying attention. I was missing out on the whole experience.

There were times during the first month or so of the girls' lives that felt disturbingly like one of those dreams.

Once, when the girls were a little over a week old, Alastair and I slipped out for a (very) quick dinner while my parents stayed with the girls. And suddenly there we were, back at one of our favorite restaurants, surrounded primarily by young, childless adults—the sort we'd been a mere days earlier. It felt frighteningly normal and natural. Whereas the fact that we had two tiny babies back home waiting for us—and not going anywhere for the foreseeable future—seemed utterly bizarre and surreal.

Another time, Alastair suggested—insisted, actually—that I go out to my favorite coffee shop and relax for an hour or so. Read a book, write in my journal. I did, and what I wrote was:

> *It's nice to get out, but it just feels like me. And what I really want is to feel like a mother. I want to feel like I'm doing something more than just fumbling and stumbling hazily through these days. I want to feel it. Maybe I'm not capable of feeling maternal. Maybe I'm so entrenched in my independence and love of things verbal and cerebral that I'll never love my girls as much as I ought to.*

Love.

Here was the crux of it: I had expected to feel a powerful, all-consuming love for these babies the minute they were born. Women talked about this all the time: how they fell for their babies instantly and rapturously and spent hours just gazing at them. But I was not one of those women, and it was a great source of guilt for me. Yes, my girls were precious to me, and, yes, if anyone had tried to harm them, I would have taken their knees out with a shotgun. But they didn't quite feel like *mine.*

Perhaps it was in part because there were two of them. Perhaps because while I was holding or "gazing" at one baby, I was always distracted, however subtly, by the presence or needs of the other, so I couldn't really, truly focus. And then there was the issue of time—twice as much of it spent nursing and changing and bathing and the rest. And the fact that we were doubly exhausted.

I also wonder if one baby feels more singularly spectacular to its parents somehow. They think, *wow.* This is *it.* This is *the* baby we created! Whereas for us, there was the strange (though no less fascinating) sensation that, wow, we could, theoretically, make a whole bunch of these things, and each one would come out slightly different. Which isn't to say that we didn't find them each individually special and precious. But we didn't fixate on them the way I think some singleton parents do with their first baby, singular.

During those first weeks, well-meaning friends and relatives with older or grown kids of their own told us repeatedly to "treasure every minute of this time—it's so precious."

And I would say that I knew, and I really was trying, really. "But," I'd add, "I can't help looking forward to when I can have an actual *relationship* with them, you know?"

If I could change the workings of the space-time continuum, I'd set it up so that you could do the newborn thing *after* you've gotten to know your babies for a while. You'd start with a five- or six-month-old, take care of them until they're twelve, maybe eighteen months. Then you'd somehow go back, give birth, and do the first three months, knowing: this is crazy, silly Clio, who's going to give me big, open-mouthed, slurpy kisses on my cheeks. And this is joyful, intrepid Elsa, who's going to fearlessly, jubilantly explore every corner of the house as soon as she can crawl. It would have made it so much easier for me to feel that all-powerful love and to cherish those newborn days, like everyone told me to.

But, the space-time continuum being what it is, all I could do is have faith that I would get to know these small strange creatures that had appeared in my life. They would work their way into my heart and my soul, and eventually I would, indeed, be not just fond of them, but madly in love with them, just like everyone said I would be.

. . .

The most frequent piece of advice we got from other parents of twins when we were expecting was to get as much help as possible—from family and friends, babysitters, passersby, whomever. We probably didn't need quite as much as the average new parents of twins do since both of us worked part-time (being artsy-fartsy layabouts has its advantages), but we still gladly accepted help when it was offered.

After a couple of visits from Phyllis, we realized—and she concurred—that what would be more useful for us was some overnight help every once in a while. So we shifted gears—and applied Alastair's parents' generosity to a different source of help: six visits from the Bluebirds, an overnight nanny service specializing in twins. This was no small gift. One night with the Bluebirds cost the equivalent of a three-star hotel in a major metropolitan area. But felt more like five-star in sheer luxuriance.

The first night a Bluebird showed up—the girls were probably three, four weeks old—it was seven o'clock, and we were hanging out in the living room per usual, the girls lounging in their bouncy seats while Alastair and I finished our dinner in front of *The Daily Show*. Our Bluebird that night was a woman in her twenties wearing comfy, well-worn sweats but managing to look authoritative in them, like a college women's swim team coach, or a dorm RA. She swept in with a cheerful hello, dimmed the lights, and told us to turn the TV volume down. Like, waaay down.

"At this time of day they're very overstimulated," she told us. "Even though they're too young for sleep training, you want to start establishing now that seven o'clock is bedtime, and wind things down."

Well then.

She took from her bag a three-ring binder filled with pre-printed charts for documenting how much and when the girls ate, how long they slept, and how many diapers they went through—all the same stuff we'd been recording in our spiral notebook. But this was much nicer and more organized look-ing, with a single page for each day. (Brilliant! Why hadn't we thought of that?)

Next, she presented us with two very small stuffed animals, a duck and a dog, with pacifiers attached.

"Cute!" I said. (*Strange,* I thought.)

"Just wait," the Bluebird said.

Little did we know that these goofy things—WubbaNubs as they're called—would be our salvation, and our daughters' most prized possessions for the next two and a half years. The advan-tage of the attached plush animals was that they kept the pacifiers from tumbling constantly out of the girls' mouths (and then roll-ing under the furniture) and, later, gave them something soft to hang on to.

When Elsa was six or seven months old, she started making a very funny noise whenever she had hers in her mouth—a gut-tural sort of sound that was roughly "goy-goy-goy." Like a Yid-dish Popeye. Then she started "asking" for it by making that sound. And so the things became known in our house as goy-goys, which eventually morphed to ga-ga.

And let me interject here just to say that pacifiers were one of those things—along with cloth diapers and no TV before two years old—that we might have attempted with one baby but that we totally cried "twins!" on. No doubt twin babies can be and frequently are raised pacifier-free. And obviously, before the dawn of rubber and silicon nipples, they frequently were. I suspect, however, that their mothers gave them rags soaked in whiskey to chew on.

So, once we had our three-ring binder and our wacky new pacifiers and had showed our Bluebird where diapers, pumped breast milk, and other essentials were, she scooped the girls up one at a time and wrapped them in the tightest, most artful swaddles we had ever seen or ever have seen since. The girls looked like small burritos. Small *frozen* burritos—they were that tight and compact. And they fell almost immediately into what appeared to be a peaceful, waking coma.

And then, Alastair and I were sent off with orders to relax. Only we weren't quite sure what to do with ourselves. Relax? Alone? Farther than ten feet from the babies?

But once the shock had subsided, we each poured ourselves a glass of wine, went upstairs and got into our pajamas, read for a bit, talked, and then went to sleep. Such a simple evening—the kind we would enjoy regularly just a few short months later—and yet at the time it felt about as luxuriant as if we were reclining on satin pillows and eating chocolate-covered strawberries whilst having our feet sensually massaged by attractive Grecian maidens.

I did still have to get up and pump twice in the course of the night, since lactation waits for no woman. I could have chosen to nurse the girls instead, but while pumping—with the help of my hands-free pumping bra, which *every* nursing woman should have—I could read a magazine or even just close my eyes and relax to the hypnotic rhythm of the pump as it sucked and stretched my nipples to the size of Vienna sausages.

And even the pumping breaks had that special Bluebird touch: when I came out of my bedroom at the prearranged time, there was a tall glass of ice water waiting for me, as well as the pump components and storage bottles, all freshly washed. (I want to say that there was a single, long-stemmed rose there, too, but I might be embellishing the memory a touch.) Afterward, I just left the filled bottles and pump parts outside the door, and our Bluebird would flit upstairs at some point and collect them. (Alastair, of course, got to sleep through the night, the lucky bastard.)

What was really amazing—and a wee bit infuriating—about the Bluebirds was that they somehow got the girls to sleep for much longer stretches than we ever could: three-and-a-half, four, once even five hours. They got them to stay amazingly in synch, too, sleeping and waking within fifteen or twenty minutes of each other.

We tried to do everything the Bluebirds did, and everything they taught us. They were big proponents of the "Five S's" for soothing babies: sucking, swaddling, shushing, swaying, and one other I can never remember. (Salami? Square dancing?) And these did help keep the girls happy, but they weren't by any means foolproof. We also attempted the Bluebird burrito-swaddles, but could never get them quite as tight. And try as we might, we just couldn't get the girls to sleep more than three hours at a stretch. Not until they were a few months older, anyway.

We joked that maybe, while we were upstairs, dead to the world, the Bluebirds turned on the oven, blew out the pilot light, and gave the girls a quick gas hit. Either that or they were using whiskey-soaked rags.

It was right around the six-week mark that I felt myself emerging from my larval mother stage.

By then, I'd lost most of my pregnancy weight—let's hear it for double nursing—my boobs weren't quite as absurdly porno-esque, and things were more or less back to normal down below. My body, while changed, felt more like mine again. Six weeks was also when breast-feeding started to feel much more second nature. I didn't have to wear the fembot plastic nipples anymore and the girls latched on easily. Nursing sessions were a whole lot shorter, so it didn't feel like such a huge time suck (ha ha). Life was certainly still challenging and round-the-clock intense. But I think the shock of what had happened had subsided a bit. I was finding my legs under me. Mother legs.

It was at just over six weeks that we got our first smiles. And all of a sudden my little larvae started to feel like my daughters. That mad mother love I'd been waiting for finally kicked in, and, every day, I found myself falling a little bit deeper. I felt *hungry* for the girls, in a surprisingly physical way. I loved holding and kissing them, cupping their little feet in my hands, pressing their increasingly soft and chubby cheeks against mine.

But because nothing is ever quite as simple with twins, of course there was a bit of a wrinkle here as well: Elsa smiled first.

One of them had to, right? The chances that the two of them would start smiling at exactly the same time—or even within a few days of each other—were miniscule. But the fact is that Elsa smiled first, Clio didn't seem anywhere close, and so we did what I suspect most new parents of twins would: we panicked.

No sooner had we started rejoicing and snapping photos and figuring out which goofy faces and sounds were most likely to win one of Elsa's gleeful, crinkly nosed smiles than we were diagnosing Clio with neurological disorders, autism, blindness, and oxygen deprivation at birth. It didn't help that nearly two weeks later she *still* wasn't smiling or even really making eye contact.

And when we brought this to our pediatrician's attention at the girls' eight-week checkup, she told us—after sort of nodding thoughtfully—that this was "still within the range of normal."

Still within the range?? When did the range end? Were we really within it, or clinging to the edge? And what did that thoughtful nodding mean?

Even more troubling than the thought that something might be wrong with Clio was the fact that, as a result of Elsa's eye contact and smiles, I felt suddenly closer to her than I did to her sister.

Alastair and I had gotten into the habit of making a stupid joke, where he would ask me, "Which baby do you like better?" Meaning it, of course, completely in jest, and completely rhetorically.

I'd usually say "the other one" or "the one who's not pooping."

But one day, shortly after Elsa had started smiling, he made the joke—"which baby do you like better?"—and I told him to shut up; I was tired of this routine.

"Because you like one of the babies better," he said, still joking.

"No," I said, and found myself suddenly on the brink of tears. "Because I feel like I know Elsa better now, and she knows me, and I feel like Clio's far away where I can't reach her and so I don't feel as connected to her. And I feel terrible about it."

All along, this had been one of my greatest fears about having twins: that I would feel closer to one than the other. And now it felt like it was happening. And maybe because I'd felt this connection with Elsa sooner, Clio would always be playing catch up.

"Baby," Alastair said, "Clio's going to smile. And you'll feel connected with her then, too."

"But are you feeling the same thing?"

"Well," he said thoughtfully, "I don't know. I sort of feel like

I get Clio. I almost respect her for not jumping into smiling too soon. I get the sense she's really thinking things over."

This made me laugh. Especially since Alastair is the same way, in many respects: a little on the shyer, more reserved side. But I wondered, will it always be this way? Will he "get" Clio—who also happens to have his brown eyes and who everyone says is the spitting image of him—and I'll "get" Elsa (whose blue eyes look just like mine), and each of us will be closer to one than the other?

To my relief, this has proved not to be the case at all. While, as it turns out, Elsa is like me in many ways—both physically and temperamentally—there's plenty that I connect with Clio on, too. I love them differently, but absolutely equally. I've also gotten used to the fact that there *are* times when I feel closer to one than the other. But the pendulum always swings back the other way sooner or later.

Clio did, of course, start to smile, at around ten weeks. Which is on the later side, but, yes, entirely within the range of normal. And—to my utter delight—her first smiles were for me.

I was changing her diaper, looking down at her on the changing table from a safe distance, and singing some kind of little nonsense song along the lines of "doo-ba doo-ba dickety-dee! Doo-ba doo-ba dickety dee!" when a smile broke slowly over her face—a dawning recognition, as if inside her small baby brain she was thinking, *wait a second, hey, that's actually pretty funny stuff.* I sang the song again, and she rewarded me with another, wider smile.

In retrospect, given Clio's temperament and personality, it makes perfect sense that these were the conditions she needed for her first smiles: she's easily overwhelmed by new and intense situations (being new to Earth most definitely counts as an intense situation). And she needs space, physical and otherwise, before she feels comfortable. So the fact that we were constantly, desperately goo-gooing and grinning right up in her face in an attempt to get her to smile—(hey, it worked with Elsa)—probably did more harm than good.

Clio's smiles turned out to be quite different from her sister's. Whereas Elsa's were guileless and delighted, Clio's had a twinkle of recognition in them—like she was in on the joke. And both smiles were equally wonderful to behold: one quintessentially Elsa and the other 100 percent Clio.

6

By the time Elsa and Clio were two months old, I was itching to jump back into work on my novel. And when they were just over three months, and it was time for me to go back to work, I was ready. Even looking forward to it.

Here, again, was something about my new life that I had not anticipated: specifically, the fact that it wasn't really a "new" life to the extent that I thought it would be. I guess I thought (and feared, a little) that I'd become unrecognizable to myself once my girls were born, that I'd be subsumed by their nonstop needs and wants and overcome with a big, fat, motherly passion for them that would crowd out any desire I had to do things like write or work or drip with sarcasm, as I am wont to do.

But, no, here I was. Still me. But with babies—babies who hadn't crowded anything out of my heart. They just fit right in there with everything else.

But because I am prone to guilt (really, a terrible flaw—I feel awful about it), this realization that I really did want to get back to work inspired a healthy dose of guilt in me. Which doesn't make rational sense, because I certainly believe that women should, if they desire, pursue their interests and career goals after having children. And I'd always planned to do just that.

Still, I didn't think I'd be quite so eager.

My feelings about the issue were undoubtedly complicated by the fact that my mother, like many of her generation, was a full-time mom and homemaker for most of my childhood. She threw herself passionately into the job, in true, earthy, seventies style. She made all our baby food from scratch—nothing out of packages or jars, unless we were away from home. Cloth diapers, no formula—of course. She even made some of our clothes herself. When we were older, it was always handmade Halloween costumes, nothing store-bought. She was an active volunteer with our schools from nursery through middle school and threw the coolest birthday parties in town.

When I think back on all this, I don't think: what a shame that she didn't do more with herself. I think: how wonderful that she was such an active, engaged, and creative mother. And then I think: is it strange or wrong that I don't really want to be the same kind of mother she was? At least, not full-time?

Not that I had a choice.

That's what's so stupid about all of this. I *had* to go back to work. But I thought that I shouldn't want to, like other working mothers I knew or had heard about—the ones who were weepy for weeks after their return to work.

I didn't weep. But it definitely was strange at first, emerging from our all-babies-all-the-time world into one where I was expected not to make jokes about poop.

Soon enough, though, I fell back into the rhythm of work: going to kickoff meetings and creative presentations, brainstorming ideas with art directors, making chitchat at the coffee machine *(Hey, need any milk in your coffee? Step right up! Ha! Ha! No? Sorry.)*, and trying really hard not to stab my hand with a ballpoint pen when clients insisted that I cram their ad copy full of words like "leverage," "enable," and "innovative."

I enjoyed the feeling of control I had at work, so different from the messiness (literal and figurative) of life back home: the order of my (mostly) neat desk, my scheduled meetings and prioritized to-do list. For a while, every Monday morning felt a little like the first day of school—preceded by extensive outfit planning, giddy anticipation, and gung-ho resolve to be organized and productive.

But I did miss the girls, and by the end of the workday on Tuesday, it was a relief knowing that Wednesday and Thursday would only be half days and that Friday I wouldn't go into work at all. I felt extremely fortunate to be able to work part-time.

The most bothersome part of my return to work was pumping. In retrospect, I guess I was sort of insane to attempt to pump for twins. It was doubly insane given the fact that the agency I worked at had an open floor plan. This was meant to enable collaboration and leverage innovation. It also meant that there were few walls and even fewer doors in the place. And the conference rooms all had windows. So the only place for me to pump was a little hidden room in the far corner of the office with a sink and a shower, intended for people who planned to exercise before or during the workday but that pretty much nobody knew about. There wasn't room for a chair, so I had to sit on the little wooden step in front of the shower stall, while a weak fluorescent ceiling lamp full of dead bugs buzzed overhead. It was a lovely environment in which to bring my wholesome, life-giving milk into the world.

Fortunately, I had that hands-free pumping bra, which meant that I could bring my laptop in and continue to work. I even got a wireless signal, which led to a few interesting little exchanges: I'd reply to an e-mail from an account manager; then he or she would stop by my desk to follow up, and I wouldn't be there, and the person would e-mail back, "Stopped by to discuss, but I must have just missed you! Swing by when you have a minute." Sure thing. I'll swing by as soon as these small bottles attached by suction to my boobs are full.

What was even more uncomfortable than crouching in a shower stall to pump, though, was the Walk of Shame between two rows of workstations—all but one of them occupied by men—on my way to the shower room, my breasts engorged and ready for business. Now, even as a woman, if I saw someone walking past my desk two or three times a day with her breast pump, knowing what she was heading off to do, I'd *pro*bably on one of those occasions find myself speculating what this pumping operation and/or her breasts looked like—probably against my own will.

Given what I think I know about the way men's minds work, I therefore suspect that on any given day there was a decent chance that at least one of my male colleagues gave a passing thought to my boobs.

I am not trying to flatter myself here. I think even if I were the most grotesquely unattractive woman on earth, this would be the case. Nor am I trying to suggest that my coworkers are in any way sleazy or reprehensible. They're perfectly nice guys. But they are guys.

Maybe it was all in my head. Maybe nobody gave a rat's ass about me or my boobs. But I still found the whole pumping-at-work operation awkward. And there were times when I had to go to ridiculous extremes to make it happen: once I had to bring my pump with me to an off-site new business pitch an hour's drive from the office and ask our client contact (female, thank God) to help me find a place to use it before the meeting, to avoid a painful engorgement and/or embarrassing leakage situation. She was very polite about it, though clearly flustered by this unexpected presentation requirement. I think I ended up pumping in a handicapped bathroom—the only enclosed space with an outlet that she could find on short order.

We didn't win that pitch.

But despite the awkwardness and inconvenience, I pumped until the girls were a year old, albeit less frequently as time went on (we started supplementing with formula, and soon after that the girls started eating solid food, too).

I have absolutely no regrets about nursing my girls for as long as I did and am glad I took the trouble to pump for them at work. But I am also absolutely sure that the sheer turbo-suction power of that pump is responsible for the fact that my breasts are now significantly smaller than they were before I had children, with bigger nipples.

See, now you're trying to picture them, too.

It was soon after my return to work, when the girls were just shy of four months old, that we first experienced the Twin Yang phenomenon. (That's my own superclever moniker for it. It's not an officially recognized phenomenon as far as I'm aware.)

Clio was going through an incredibly difficult phase—difficult for me, that is—with regard to nursing. Every time I tried to nurse her, she'd start screaming and arching her back, sometimes before I even got her latched on. The only way she'd relent and eat was if I gave her a bottle of expressed milk.

Had Elsa also been rejecting the breast, I might have given in and just started bottle-feeding both of them. But Elsa was at that point the world's biggest fan of mom's boobs. I hated the idea of nursing her—continuing to have that special, physical closeness and cuddle time—while bottle-feeding Clio. Not that bottle feeding couldn't be cuddly in its own way. It was the contrast that bothered me. I didn't want to go from nestling Elsa against my bare skin and having her drink milk from my own body to giving Clio a plastic bottle of milk extracted from my milk ducts by a machine.

At the same time, I hated feeling like I was in a battle of wills with my daughter. I hated the fact that she was (seemingly) rejecting me like this. And I hated how angry it made me—how, during those screaming, back-arching fits she had, I sometimes actually found myself thinking, about my own, four-month-old baby, *Dammit, what is your* problem? *Why are you being such a* jerk?

And what if this was going to be our relationship? Was my daughter going to be like a perpetual, rebellious, and not-very-nice teenager from here on out? Were her first words going to be, "I didn't ask to be born!"?

At my wits' end, I called my local chapter of the La Leche League—a nonprofit organization with chapters all over the country dedicated to supporting women who are breast-feeding. The volunteer I spoke to suggested that the root of the problem could be the fact that Clio was getting accustomed to having bottles while I was at work and was having difficulty transitioning back and forth.

I started to say, "but my other daughter isn't having any

trouble," and then realized that this was about as relevant as the fact that I'd had Raisin Bran for breakfast. Elsa was a different person.

The volunteer suggested that I express a little bit of milk before putting Clio onto the breast, to make sure that the milk wasn't coming out at her like a fire hose at the initial letdown (something that bottles don't do). She also suggested that I try giving her some breast milk in a medicine cup. This seemed absurd. Was I supposed to spend the next year feeding my infant daughter with a cup?

"No," the woman explained. "It's basically just to annoy her, so she realizes she has no choice but to go back to nursing."

And as predicted, Clio was annoyed by the cup. Incredibly so. Which only made it harder to get her to calm down and nurse. The only thing that seemed to work, and only some of the time, was to bounce her up and down on the exercise ball, singing madly (once, I hummed the entirety of Mozart's *Eine Kleine Nachtmusik*) until she stopped yelling and let her body relax. Then I would lie down on my side, lay her down close to me, and offer my breast up to her like it was a passed hors d'oeuvre. *Milk, in a breasty sort of pastry shell? No? Yes? Here, have a cocktail napkin.*

It was exhausting having to go through this little dance every time I tried to feed her. And she was being fussy and difficult in general, not just while nursing.

Meanwhile, Elsa was being "your sister." As in, "why can't you be more like your sister?" She was good-natured and even-tempered, smiley and pleasant, like clockwork when it came to eating and pooping. She nursed with gusto, and was so good at it that I could even walk around the house with her on my boob. In short, she was a joy.

"Well, at least *she's* in a good mood," Alastair and I said to each other more than once during this phase.

And then suddenly, a week or two later, Clio was the one vying for Baby of the Year. She was smiling and gurgling and cooing with abandon, her small mouth working over all manner of guttural syllables. She slept better at night. Best of all, I no longer had to spend fifteen minutes helping her pull herself together before every feeding and then lie on my side like a collie to nurse her.

But now—you guessed it—Elsa was the one being a drama queen. She didn't have the same nursing issues as Clio, but she was fussy and ornery, spitting up more than usual and sleeping shorter intervals at night. She was in no mood for prolonged smiling and googly eyes; she wanted to sit in her bouncy seat and bat sullenly at its dangling plastic toys while emitting the occasional whiney grunt.

Classic Twin Yang.

We saw it happen again and again over the next three years: one of the girls would be in a particularly miserable phase and the other would be particularly pleasant, and then, almost without warning, they'd switch. There was in-between, too, of course, when the girls' moods were a mixed bag. There were also times when both of them were being particularly challenging or particularly delightful. But we were always surprised at how much Twin Yang there was, and how dramatic it could be.

I've talked with other parents of twins about this phenomenon, which they've witnessed in their twins as well. We like to come up with crackpot scientific theories as to why it happens: Is it a subconscious balancing out that they perform, as if to keep their twin organism in homeostasis? Or when one of them is feeling particularly stable and happy, does the other somehow feel like she has permission to be needy? And is it self-imposed, or does it have to do with the way we, their parents, react to them? Is the "good" twin, in fact, trying to cut us a break?

The funny thing about Twin Yang is that it's both a negative and a positive from a parental standpoint: when you're dealing with one needy child, at least you get a bit of a break with the other one. But when you've got one really happy and pleasant child, you can't fully enjoy and appreciate—or even reward—her mood, because you're too busy dealing with her needy sibling. She's being an angel, and yet she gets the shaft. So maybe the bad behavior is a cry for more attention. Maybe this is how twins vie for the one-on-one time they crave.

So much of life with twins is Twin Yang–esque. For every pro (two kids in one fell swoop!), there's a con (two in college at the same time!). For every advantage (they'll be lifelong friends!), there's a disadvantage (they fight like drunken sailors!). For every yin, a yang.

7

Back when I was six or seven months pregnant, Alastair and I went to a dinner party hosted by my friend Mandy and her husband—the ones with twin girls a couple of years older than ours.

When we arrived, shortly after seven, I was shocked to see that the twins—who would have been two at the time—were nowhere in sight. Except for the toys tucked neatly away here and there, you would never have even known that there were children in the house, let alone a pair of two-year-olds. Classical music played over the stereo, candles were lit in the hall, and the dining room table was elegantly set.

As nice as it was, I was actually a little disappointed; I hadn't seen their girls since I'd found out that I was having twin girls of my own. I was looking forward to seeing them and perhaps getting a glimpse of what our life might be like when our own daughters-to-be were their age.

"Are they with grandparents for the weekend?" I asked.

"Oh no," Mandy said. "They're in bed."

I couldn't believe it: two-year-old twins, and here she and her husband were, hosting a completely sophisticated, grown-up dinner party? "Do they always go to bed this early?" I asked. "What time do they get up?"

"We get them to bed at seven, and they get up at seven in the morning, give or take."

"Wow," I said. "That's amazing." I had never thought such a thing was possible.

"You'll get there with yours, too," she assured me. As if there wasn't any question about it. "It's so important. Not just for them, but for your own sanity."

And by the time Elsa and Clio were around five months old, we had at least succeeded in getting them onto a mostly coordinated two-naps-a-day schedule—a long one in the morning and a shorter one in the afternoon. But nighttime was another thing altogether. Sure, we were putting them to bed at seven. But getting them to sleep all the way until 7:00 A.M. (with or without a lovely dinner party in between) was still a very far, distant dream.

It didn't help that we couldn't find any sleep techniques or books aimed specifically at twins (I think there are a couple on the market now, you lucky expecting-twins people out there). In the books we did have, the challenge of getting multiples to sleep through the night in the same room merited only a few pages, and the advice was more or less, "the same techniques for a single baby work for two babies, except, of course, there's the chance that one baby will wake the other one up, so crying it out might not work. And there's also a chance that they'll have different sleep patterns and needs. So, um, good luck with that."

Other parents of twins didn't have much in the way of practical advice to offer either, just encouragement. "Stick to your guns," they told us. "It *can* be done."

Our primary strategy was to be as consistent as possible. So in theory, our nights went like this: I nursed the babies between 6:00 and 7:00 P.M., got them in clean diapers and sleepers, read them a story (just because), and turned on the vacuum cleaner CD.

The what? you ask. Yes. We had a CD of a vacuum cleaner on a continuous loop. I discovered the power of the vacuum quite by accident one day, while vacuuming in the living room—it might actually have been the *only* time I vacuumed the living room in the first year of the girls' lives. They were being fussy and whiney, and I think I started cleaning in part because I'd had it with them. Once I turned the vacuum on, they immediately calmed down, and eventually drifted off to sleep. Thinking I'd better stop, so they'd stay asleep, I turned the vacuum off. Cry-ville. So, back on it went: Sleepytown.

The living room got damned clean that day.

Since running the vacuum in the girls' bedroom all night didn't seem like a particularly practical or earth-friendly option, Alastair found an MP3 of a vacuum cleaner online—proof that you can find absolutely anything on the Internet—and burned back-to-back tracks of it onto CD.

We wore out three vacuum cleaner CDs and one portable CD player before the girls were eighteen months old, and we had the good sense to finally buy a white-noise machine. In fact, I'm not really sure why we didn't get a white-noise machine from the get-go. I guess we were superstitious. You find something that works, you don't want to mess with it.

In any case, once the vacuum CD was deployed and the lights turned off, tummies rubbed, the girls would usually fall asleep fairly quickly. At 10:30 P.M., after I'd pumped and gone to bed, Alastair would give them a "dream feed" bottle—breast milk or formula—trying not to wake them in the process. They'd wake up again a few hours later, and I would nurse them, then nurse them again at 6:30ish, before I got ready for work. Occasionally, Elsa—who has always been and continues to be a little heavier than Clio—would skip the middle-of-the night feeding altogether, and when this happened we felt like life was beautiful; the universe was guided by a benevolent, unseen hand; and world peace was attainable in our lifetime.

Of course, the best-case scenario above doesn't take into account disastrous diapers, unexplained crying fits (Clio), voracious hunger during growth spurts (Elsa), or middle-of-the-night fuzzy logic and temporary dementia (Alastair/me).

Once when the girls were just over five months old, Alastair was out playing a late gig, so instead of giving the girls their customary bottle of formula at 10:30, I decided to nurse them. But I didn't have a great milk supply late at night, and they tended to digest it faster than formula, so Clio woke up three hours later wanting to be fed again.

But before resorting to feeding her—because we'd vowed, as we vowed most nights, to see if we could get the babies to sleep longer stretches—Alastair, who'd only recently come home, tried to bounce with her on the fitness ball in the nursery to soothe her back to sleep. Fifteen minutes later, she was still crying—nay, screaming—so I got up and went to the nursery, prepared to give her the ole boob. What followed was a dialogue along these lines:

> **Me:** She may just be hungry, since she didn't have formula tonight. I should probably just nurse her.
>
> **A:** What? I can't hear you.

(The fan is on, as well as the vacuum cleaner CD: I'm whispering so as not to wake Elsa; and Clio, of course, is screaming. Man, that girl could scream.)

Me: She didn't have FORMULA so she's probably HUNGRY. Maybe I should just NURSE her.

A: (unintelligible)

Me: What?

A: (rolls eyes and motions for me to come closer) It's really EARLY. I thought we were going to try to PUSH them!

Me: Yeah, I guess we should. The other night they didn't have formula either, and they slept.

A: But it's hotter tonight. They're probably too hot. Wait, how long has it been since they ate?

Me (counting on fingers): Four hours. No, three. Wait, what time is it?

A: Around two, I think.

Me: Do you want to bring Clio into our bedroom? Elsa's going to wake up.

A: But then you won't be able to sleep.

(At this point, Elsa starts crying.)

Both of us in unison: Shit!

I bend over the crib to see if Elsa has come unswaddled—we were pushing the limits of the time frame for swaddling at that point, by using a secret Bluebird double-blanket swaddling method that I cannot reveal.

A: Did she come unswaddled?

Me: Yeah, but she probably just woke up because of Clio. Or maybe she's cold. Her legs feel cold. Maybe

I should put a sleeper on her. Why did you turn the fan back on?

A: It was really hot. Turn it off if you think it's too cold.

Me: No, it's fine, it's fine.

At this point, Clio takes it up a notch, Elsa starts whimpering again, and I'm still standing there, immobile and half-asleep, debating whether to put a sleeper on her or unswaddle her so she can stick her hands in her mouth, or both. Someone—the cat?—has turned off the fan.

A: Here, you feed Clio, and I'll take care of Elsa. Do you want me to put a sleeper on her?

Me: I don't know. I'm afraid it will wake her up. (I take Clio from him.) Do you think maybe she's just teething? She keeps sticking her hand in her mouth.

A: Elsa?

Me: No, Clio.

A: I don't know. (He puts a sleeper on Elsa, and in so doing discovers she's soaked through her diaper, so he changes her, which wakes her up completely.)

Me: I guess I should feed Elsa, too, as long as she's awake.

A: Maybe she'll go back to sleep now that I changed her. Should I try to put her back down?

Me: I don't know. Maybe we should put the fan back on now that she's in a sleeper?

A: I don't know!

Me: I don't know either!

A: There are too many variables!

Me: I hate math!

Me & A (in unison): AaaagGGggHhhhGHHGHHhh-
GGhhh!!!

We probably could have been more aggressive in our sleep training. But it's not easy to do the whole cry-it-out thing (or even use the modified cry-it-out approach, which we did) when (a) you're afraid that one baby is going to wake the other one up and (b) you're exhausted and not thinking straight and all you want to do is take the most expedient route back to sleep for both the babies and yourself.

So the girls held onto that middle-of-the-night feeding until they were almost seven months old. Around that time, I called the director of the Bluebirds—once a Bluebird customer, always a Bluebird customer—and she told me sternly, in her British accent, which made it sound even sterner, "they do *not* need that feeding! They should absolutely be sleeping through the night!"

I uttered something along the lines of, "Yes, ma'am."

Lady Bluebird then instructed me to gradually taper the amount of time I nursed the girls or the amount of milk or formula I gave them, and then let them cry it out if necessary beyond that. It worked in a matter of days—Bluebird magic once again—and the 4:00 A.M. feeding was no more.

And I realized that, in truth, I had probably been the one holding on to that last feeding. I didn't particularly like dragging myself out of bed in darkness, but I didn't mind sitting there in the rocker in the corner of the nursery, quietly nursing Elsa and then Clio, listening to their soft sounds, cradling their soft heads and breathing in the scent of them while the rest of the world slept.

By the time they were eight months old, the ten o'clock feeding was gone too, and they were sleeping from—yes—seven at night to roughly seven in the morning. Plus two naps a day, until they were fourteen months old. At almost three years old, they were still sleeping twelve hours a night, with the occasional afternoon nap.

I can't resist mentioning here that a lot of our good friends had their first child (singular) around the same time we had our girls. Our newborn nights were surely twice as hellish as theirs. But guess whose babies ended up being the more disciplined and predictable sleepers in the long run? Yep.

I suspect that some of our friends and acquaintances thought we were uptight crazies for planning our lives around the girls' nap schedule and insisting on putting them down to bed every night, in their own cribs, at seven o'clock sharp. We knew of plenty of singleton parents who toted their babies around at all hours, letting them fall asleep whenever and wherever they felt like it.

But when those rock and roll babies hit the one-year mark and still weren't sleeping through the night, were cranky and over-tired for lack of naps, or refused to fall asleep anywhere but in their parents' beds, several of our friends sheepishly asked us: um, how did you do it?

Maybe we just got lucky with our girls, and they're naturally good sleepers. But our three couple friends with twins *also* have so-called good sleepers. I don't think it's a coincidence. When you've got twins, you don't mess around with sleep routines. You can't, or you'll never have a moment's rest yourself.

Which isn't to say that it's easy, but it can be done. Stick to your guns. You may even end up the envy of your singleton parent friends.

. . .

Oh, but there were times during that first year when I was so
envious of my singleton parent friends. I'd see a new mother
walking around Davis Square with a baby snuggled against her
chest in a BabyBjörn or tucked into a svelte little stroller, ducking
into shops or having coffee with a friend—while I strode pur-
posefully by with my girls in their hulking double stroller, attempting to enjoy a walk, but all the while praying we'd make
it back home before one or both of them needed a diaper change
(a double stroller doesn't fit into your average public restroom, so
what do you do with the second baby while you're changing the
first?) or needed to be fed again (what if, while giving a bottle to
or discreetly nursing one, the other started to holler?).

I have always prized my independence, particularly when it
comes to being out and about in the world. In my twenties I traveled alone extensively—in Cameroon, Guatemala, South America, and elsewhere. There's nothing I find quite as liberating or
pleasurable as exploring an unfamiliar place or even just strolling
through a familiar one on my own. I've been doing it since I was
a kid, taking long, solo bike rides around my hometown (sans hel-
met, of course, because one could back then) and playing Dun-
geons and Dragons–esque text adventures on our Apple IIE,
searching for secret passageways and keys to locked doors.

So I would have appreciated the opportunity to ease gradually out of my lone-wolf tendencies with one small, snuggly,
and relatively portable passenger along for the ride. Instead, my
wings were clipped right there in the delivery room. And sure, a
baby clips everyone's wings. But mine felt clipped-er.

What made it harder was that so many people just didn't get

it. They didn't realize how complicated it was to get out or spend time in an unfamiliar environment with two babies in tow.

When the girls were about five months old, I went to the baby shower of some good friends. Alastair was out of town, so I had our sitter—a middle-aged woman with grown kids of her own, whom we'd hired to look after the girls about twelve hours a week—come for the afternoon. I looked forward to the shower all week: the opportunity to wear something nice and un-milk-stained, make conversation with other adults, and have both of my hands free. (Perhaps even to hold an adult beverage!)

I pumped right before I went, buying myself a good three hours of freedom. It was a beautiful spring day, and the drive there, to the lovely Boston suburb of Wellesley, was gorgeous: big old houses, budding trees, flowers in bloom. It was, on a small scale, something of an adventure.

But when I walked into the house, I was greeted with: Where are the twins? Why didn't you bring the twins? Oh, we were hoping to meet the twins!

And I'm thinking: are you *insane*? Come to someone else's house, alone, with two five-month-olds? What would be the point? I might as well just not come at all, for all the attention I'd be able to give to anyone or anything else at the party.

What I ended up saying, with a smile, was: "Well, if I'd brought them, I wouldn't be able to talk to you right now."

"Oh, but we would have helped!" they all said.

And maybe they would have. But usually when people say they'll help with babies, it means holding them while they sleep or gurgle happily, and then handing them back to their parents when they get fussy or hungry or need a diaper change, which is, of course, when you need help the most.

Even going places with the girls together with Alastair, though not quite as stressful, was tough. We took walks, hit some museums, and a few times attempted a meal or a cup of coffee out. But in these last instances, we would often find ourselves looking longingly, and a touch spitefully, at the other couples with their one baby propped up on the table in a car seat, or being passed back and forth between them while they took turns eating. You don't get to take turns with twin infants.

Know what you do get, though? Attention. *Tons* of it.

What is it about twins that people find so fascinating and adorable? I think I might have known before I had them myself, but now that twins—my twins—are part of my everyday reality, it's hard to say.

Well, that's not quite true. To see them bundled up, sleeping side by side as newborns, was awfully sweet. And when, later, as toddlers, they sometimes walked holding hands, it was so sweet it nearly made my teeth ache.

So maybe it's the inferred fondness and affection between two babies—this sense that they are in love and in cahoots with each other—that's part of the charm. Or maybe it's just math: one baby is cute. Two babies, twice as cute. Plus, an affection for symmetry seems to be hardwired into us as humans. (Which is part of why identical twins inspire even more gawking than fraternal ones, from what I've heard.) But more than anything, it's probably just the exoticness factor. Although the twin birthrate in the developed world continues to climb, twins are still relatively rare, and always will be.

Still, I was kind of floored by just how much attention we got when we were out and about with the girls. The "twinlookers" generally fell into two categories: there was the benign and relatively unobtrusive sort—people who would smile fondly and ask a few questions. The first was usually "twins?" (Which I found very odd at first because, well, *duh*. But I guess I could, conceivably, have been taking care of a friend or relative's baby along with my own. Or the girls could have been siblings verrrry close in age, Elsa always being a little bit bigger than Clio.)

The next question tended to be "are they identical or fraternal?" Or, sometimes, entertainingly, "paternal or maternal?"

Sometimes people asked the girls' ages and names, and if they left it at that, it was great. I felt mildly flattered by the attention, and could go about whatever it was I was doing—very likely trying to get home to nurse the girls before they started melting down.

But then there were the twinlookers who just kept on going.

For Alastair's first-ever Father's Day, I gave him tickets to an Edward Hopper exhibition at the Museum of Fine Arts. When the girls were very tiny, we'd successfully brought them to two museums in Boston, so I thought that a museum outing would be a great thing for us to do on a spring afternoon.

What I failed to take into consideration, however, was the fact that the exhibition would be very, very crowded, especially on a Saturday, which was when we went. What I also sort of ignored was the fact that, at almost six months old, the girls weren't as likely to sleep or just lie there quietly most of the time, as they had on our earlier museum outings.

To make matters worse, as it turned out, the exhibition was in a gallery with very narrow corridors. Between that and the crowds, it would have been impossible to maneuver our double stroller. And, unfortunately, we had forgotten to bring the baby carriers. (As organized as we were, in the whirlwind of trying to get out the door with everything that we and the girls needed, we often forgot something. If we were lucky, it was something of ours—a cell phone or pair of sunglasses. If we weren't so lucky, it was extra diapers or a bottle.)

We tried carrying the girls through the exhibit in our arms, but they were both in fussy, hungry moods—it was one of those days where nothing was going quite as expected with regard to the girls' eating, sleeping, and pooping patterns—so in the end, I offered to sit outside in the museum's main corridor with them so Alastair could take in the exhibition.

As I was sitting there, giving Elsa a bottle while moving the stroller back and forth with my foot to try to keep a cranky Clio quiet, a number of the people passing by smiled at us, as if we were a surprising and unexpectedly charming museum installation. Some stopped to ask "twins?" or "identical or fraternal?" It was all benign enough, although as the girls got fussier—Elsa was refusing to take her bottle—I began to get annoyed, tired of feeling like we were on display. But there was no place more private to sit, so there we were.

And then along came a middle-aged woman in an artsy, hand-knit-looking sweater, carrying a bag from the gift shop, who sat down next to me—a little closer than normal social conventions allowed—and started immediately in with the questions, as if she was ticking them off on a checklist.

After fraternal, names, and ages were established, she went right into the serious stuff: "Do they run in your family, or did you have IVF? My best friend's daughter had IVF so I know all about it. She has boy-girl twins who are three now."

I told her that, yes, we'd had fertility treatments, but not IVF. Meanwhile, Elsa still wouldn't take her bottle and was starting to cry in earnest. I took a blanket out from under the stroller and slung it over my shoulder so I could nurse her. I wasn't a huge fan of the nursing-in-public thing—it was always awkward, trying to get the blanket to stay on and being constantly nervous about inadvertently flashing boob to the world.

The fact that I was distracted by this activity didn't faze my new friend in the least. "Do they have very different personalities?" she asked. "My friend's daughter's twins are like night and day."

I told her that, yes, the girls appeared to have different personalities.

She gestured at Clio. "That one looks like she's got a mind of her own! Look out!"

At that point, Clio was lying there chewing on a ring of plastic toy keys, which I'd finally managed to distract her with. Look out, indeed!

Meanwhile, Elsa was, uncharacteristically, having trouble latching on and staying that way. Probably because I had her at a weird angle, on account of using my elbow to try to keep the blanket from slipping off my shoulder.

"Is that one always a fussy nurser?" the woman asked, motioning at Elsa's feet, sticking out from the blanket.

"Not usually," I said. "It's just always tricky nursing in public." Hint, hint.

I knew that my interviewer meant well, and she seemed like a perfectly nice, if nosy, person. But I really, really wished she would go away now.

But she didn't. "I think it's wonderful that it's become more acceptable for women to nurse in public. It wasn't that way when I had my children. You're very, very lucky."

She went on to ask me if I ever nursed them both at the same time ("so how, exactly, does that work?"), how we came up with their names, whether we ever dressed them alike, whether we planned to have more children, whether I had a C-section or not, and how much weight I gained when I was pregnant.

And then, suddenly, she looked up and waved to someone on the other side of the hall, said to me, sounding slightly annoyed, "well, that's my friend, I really have to go," and took off, as if I'd been the one keeping her there the whole time.

I don't mean to sound uncharitable. I really don't. I understand that people are curious about twins, and in fact I like the way that babies—whether single or in pairs—melt the walls between strangers in public. But when people seemed to think that the fact that I had twins gave them the right to corner and grill me with endless and sometimes very personal questions, it brought out the misanthrope in me. It made me want to say, *Look, I'm not a freak of nature here. And my children aren't either. They're just two small people that happened to be born at the same time. Get over it already.*

(Says the woman writing a book about twins.)

8

One of the much-touted awesome things about twins kicked in when the girls were six, seven, eight months old: they started truly noticing and interacting with each other. And I became our own, in-house twinlooker. Only my probing questions were more along the lines of, "Did she take your bunny? Yeah? Where's your bunny?! Do you want your bunny back? Oops! Is that your bunny??"

Because this was how it began, the complex relationship of Elsa and Clio: they'd lie under The Stimulator (now a huge hit) or sit on a blanket, side by side, and grab toys out of each other's hands and mouths. At that point it didn't seem to bother either of them much when her sister snatched what she had just been holding. ("I had the colored plastic thingy, and now the colored plastic thingy is gone. OK. I'll grab a new plastic thingy and shove it in my mouth instead.")

If we held them up face to face, they'd smile and babble at each other, then reach out and grab each other's hands/noses/mouths/

cheeks, sometimes gently and sometimes with great, violent gusto. Around this time they also discovered the joys of ear-splitting, pterodactyl-like squeaking. And while it could get to be a bit much, especially if we were out in public, some-times when they sat together grinning and squealing at each other, I was so overcome by the sweetness of it I felt like join-ing in.

One summer afternoon, in the midst of this period of prime baby cuteness, we were driving home from the first birthday party of our friends' daughter, the girls sleeping soundly in the back, having crashed out after their first-ever taste of birthday cake. I was so contented and delighted by life with babies that I said to Alastair, "You know, it might be kind of nice to have a little brother for the girls someday, wouldn't it?"

He admitted that, yes, it might. More than once lately he'd commented on how this whole twin thing wasn't quite as ex-cruciatingly hard as he had imagined it would be, and I agreed. People had made it sound like it was going to be a living hell, and it really wasn't. Tiring, sure. But so lovely. Especially now that the girls' personalities had started to emerge in full force.

"I wouldn't want to do fertility again, because we might end up with more twins," I said. "But maybe in a couple of years we could just try, and see what happens." I'd heard plenty of anec-dotes of people who'd struggled to get pregnant the first time and used fertility treatments getting pregnant on their own after having their first baby. (Sometimes quite unintentionally, as had happened to a friend of mine who unexpectedly found herself pregnant four months after her twins were born.)

"Or we could adopt," Alastair offered.

"Yeah, maybe," I said, dreamily, enjoying a sunny vision of Elsa and Clio as four- or five-year-olds, playing with and tickling a baby boy of indeterminate race with a gummy smile, adorably seven or eight months old, of course.

Less than a year later, I would remind Alastair of that conversation and ask, "What were we, high or something?"

I've since heard that the six- to twelve-month baby age is a frequent danger zone, when parents are lulled into thinking that this whole childrearing thing is a piece of cake. Amnesia with regard to labor, birth, and the first sleepless nights has, by this time, set in as well.

If you're expecting or have just had twins, and you're certain you want another child, the danger zone may be the best possible time to do it. Before they turn into toddlers and you find yourself standing in the middle of your kitchen while both of your children are screaming because you cut their sandwiches into squares instead of triangles, and not only do you never want to have another child again, ever, but you're wondering if it's too late to give yours back.

Oops. Did I just write that out loud?

By now, people had regularly started referring to me as a Mother of Twins.

"This is Jane," a friend or colleague might say when introducing me to someone else, "and she's a mother of twins!"

I always found this odd. I was a mother, yes, and gradually knitting this new part of me into my sense of self. But I didn't think of myself as a different species of mother—as other people seemed to—simply because I happened to have carried both of my children in my womb at once.

I don't mean to disparage anyone who has referred to me as a Mother of Twins or will in the future; I know it's meant in a fond, almost adulatory way. The way someone might say, "She's the first violinist in the New York Philharmonic!" or "She's an astronaut!" (Well, not *quite* like that, I guess.)

I always liked it better when people said things like, "She's a writer and a copywriter and a blogger *and* she's a mother of twins on top of all that!" Because for me, this was the real accomplishment: that I was managing to successfully mother my twins—an accomplishment in and of itself—*and* still do other things that were important to me.

At which point the person I was being introduced to would say, "Wow! Are they identical or fraternal?"

I did, however, begin to think of Mother of Twins as a subcategory of my identity. I started to own it. I think it was in large part because I was getting better and more confident in the whole stereo mothering thing. I learned to anticipate what the various challenges in any given scenario would be, even if I wasn't always able to surmount them with grace or even success. I felt less intimidated by my own children and more comfortable with (and accustomed to) chaos, in public as well as at home.

Case in point: when the girls were eight months old, I went to the grocery store with them, by myself, and didn't have a nervous breakdown in the process.

This was, in part, a training exercise. Alastair would be going on tour in Europe for a few weeks the next month, and although I would have help from parents and sitters, I would also be on my own with the girls for significant stretches of time. I wanted to be sure that I could handle doing errands with them if necessity demanded.

I planned for our outing like it was a trek in the Himalayas. Gear: backpack baby carrier, bottles, snacks, and an extremely detailed shopping list. Pretrip prep: feed babies, put on clean diapers (them), pee (me). Game plan: park right next to shopping cart return area and obtain cart; open rear door of Subaru Forester and place baby backpack at edge of cargo area; put lighter baby (Clio) in pack, squat down, and put pack on; retrieve heavier baby (Elsa) from car seat and place in seat-shelf thingy at back of shopping cart and say a brief, silent prayer of thanks to whomever it was who came up with this brilliant design innovation—perhaps some pencil-necked engineer in a skinny black tie and short-sleeved shirt, circa 1958. Love that guy.

It occurred to me somewhere in the produce section that I probably should have sanitized the handle of the cart, but I was hoping that the bacteria would cut me a break. The shopping itself wasn't that difficult. When Elsa started to get fussy, I gave her a graham cracker (the girl always was and continues to be easily placated by carbohydrates). To reach anything on the low shelves, I had to remember to squat straight down, not bend over, lest Clio go tumbling out of the backpack onto a shelf of canned goods. Above all, I had to keep moving. One does not linger thoughtfully in a grocery store, carefully scrutinizing labels and comparing prices, when one is accompanied by two small ticking time bombs in diapers.

To my great satisfaction, the trip was a success. In fact, the only thing that slowed us down was a handful of twinlookers, but they were of the most harmless sort. They just smiled and waved at the babies, asked if they were twins, and moved on. In one case, eager to practice my crapola Spanish, I was the one who struck up a conversation, with a young Spanish-speaking couple that I heard say, "*que lindas!*" as they smiled at the girls.

"*Son gemelitas!*" I said, extremely proud of the fact that I knew the word for "little twin girls." At which point the couple launched into a series of questions in rapid-fire Spanish. I could handle names and ages, but I'd never learned the Spanish words for "fraternal" and "identical," so I smiled apologetically, played the "sorry, *no entiendo*" card, and moved on to paper goods.

Every item in my list was successfully added to the cart. And once we'd made it through checkout ("identical or fraternal?") and into the parking lot, I even took a picture of the occasion, for posterity: Elsa, sitting in the carriage, with a sack of basmati rice on one side of her and jug of laundry detergent on the other. (Clio, you'll recall, was on my back.) Only I took it with my lousy, no-frills cell phone, and when I sent it to myself it was about a half-inch square, and I couldn't increase the size without it turning all blurry. But I still have it, saved on my computer: a tiny, less-than-postage-stamp-sized reminder of a very large accomplishment.

In fact, I started to sort of dig the challenge and adventure of this kind of solo outing with the girls. The times it didn't go horribly awry, that is. It was as if the part of me that used to love making packing lists and poring over *Lonely Planet* guidebooks to map out a course for my next travel adventure had found a new outlet. One that involved diapers and wipes instead of a money belt and a Swiss army knife.

When Alastair did his three-week tour in Europe, the girls were ten months old, and I had more than one opportunity to test my Adventure Mom mettle. The most memorable was the time I drove on my own with the girls for a weekend at my parents' house in Maine—a two-and-a-half-hour drive.

It sounds straightforward enough, but there were numerous potential issues to contend with—dropped pacifiers, diaper explosions, inexplicable crying (mono or stereo), general baby ennui.

But what really had me worried was what I would do if I needed to pee. I was still nursing and therefore still taking in a lot of fluids. On top of that, I was probably drinking a bit more coffee than usual to combat the fatigue of dealing with two babies on my own, continuously. I've also just got a really small bladder. So having to make a pit stop in the course of a two-and-a-half-hour trip (potentially lengthened by roadside stops to deal with various baby antics) would not have been out of the question.

By this time the girls were no longer in the kind of car seat that could be lifted out of their bases, and I hadn't brought our (gigantic) double stroller. Getting both of them out and into a public restroom would have been challenging. Not that I couldn't carry both of them at once—I could (and, damn, did my arms look good)—but it would be tough. And once I got there, where would I put them while I did my business? I could hold one, I supposed. And put the other on the—ugh—floor?

I came up with all kinds of contingency plans in case I just couldn't hold it. I could pull up to a gas station with a convenience store and run inside to see if there was some sane woman or teenage girl working there, whom I could beg to come look at the girls while I ran inside. I could try to find somewhere to pull off the road where I could go behind a bush while still keeping the car in my sight line. Or I could look for a Dunkin' Donuts, where, this being New England, I'd have a good chance of finding a cop that I could (maybe?) enlist to watch the car.

In the end, I just deprived myself of liquids. And the girls slept almost the entire time. The whole thing went off without a hitch.

Riding in the back of a pickup truck along with twelve other people and a sackful of chickens in Cameroon. Driving to Maine in a Subaru with two infants. Same basic idea.

. . .

But in the Subaru with the infants was definitely where I wanted to be.

In fact, throughout the whole first year of the girls' lives, I never felt like I was supposed to be anywhere but where I was. I looked forward to aspects of the future, of course; I was eager to hear what thoughts and ideas would issue from the girls' brains once they started talking, and I looked forward to the things we'd be able to do and share with them when they were older. But it was mostly a happy sort of looking forward, not an antsy one.

Far so much of my adult life—probably from my eighteenth birthday on—I'd always had my sights on the future. Alastair was the same way. Pre-children, we frequently took long weekend drives, often quite literally closing our eyes and pointing to a place on a map. We found ourselves in Portsmouth, Providence, Rockport, Plymouth, Gloucester, and countless other towns named centuries ago by homesick British settlers. We'd stroll and eat and drink and wander, and inevitably our conversation turned to what was next, and how we'd get there. Should I apply to MFA programs? Should he try to find a full-time job? When would we buy a house, have children, figure it all out? We felt like our current lives were a preamble to the day when we would land squarely in our life as it was meant to be.

Once the girls were born—and after I got through the initial strangeness and adjustment of the first few months—I felt like I'd landed. I was completely content and in the moment.

And I was surprised at how sanguine I felt about the changes that the girls had wrought in my life. My days and nights were fuller, messier, more intense. My "me" time was seriously curtailed. And I was frequently very, very tired. But it was all good.

All totally worth it for the joy my girls brought me—and the joy I was finding in being a parent together with Alastair.

Even the enormous amount of crap in our house didn't faze me. The entire living area and kitchen were overtaken with baby paraphernalia. The floors became gradually more cluttered with toys and stuffed animals. Our beautiful, antique, art deco sideboard—a piece from my parents' house that I'd coveted starting when I was thirteen—had been transformed into a changing table. Our couch was spit-up and breast-milk central. (I was very proud of myself for having the foresight to insist that we pay extra for the super-high-tech-stain-resistant coating.) But who cared?

Meanwhile, I loved my work-parenting-writing balance. Work stayed mostly within its boundaries of twenty-five to thirty hours a week, so Wednesday afternoons and Fridays were mine to spend with the girls. Thursday afternoons when the sitter came and nap times were novel-writing time—and the girls were excellent nappers. I was blogging now, too—when the girls were five months, I started writing my *Baby Squared* blog at Babble.com. I even managed to exercise now and then, and was close to my pre-baby weight.

I was holding it all together, doing this graceful juggling act. And I felt a sense of fulfillment that I'd never experienced before in my adult life.

And depression? I couldn't have been farther from it. I'd left the postpartum danger zone behind and was walking steadily, mindfully forward, for the most part weathering the frustrations and fatigue of twin motherhood with a healthy "this too shall pass" attitude.

I was still on my usual low dose of Prozac. I assumed that it was simply doing its job, keeping me at baseline. And the fact that I felt happier and more contented than I ever had before was a function of the circumstances of my life, and my mind-set within them. So I assumed. And maybe this assumption was correct.

But sometimes I wonder, in retrospect, if I was experiencing a slightly enhanced version of my very real happiness. Oxytocin, a pituitary hormone required for lactation, is associated with happiness, trust, and calm, and is thought to be partly responsible for the "bonding" that happens between nursing mothers and their babies. I was nursing two babies. My body was a little oxytocin factory, and maybe I was reaping the benefits. Or maybe it was something else entirely—another brew of hormones or neurotransmitters that my brain had never made or tasted before. Because, as I'd learn soon enough, there were some changes afoot in my brain chemistry.

But maybe I'm overanalyzing. Maybe I really was just happy.

9

Elsa crawled first, at almost exactly seven months. The girl crawled fast. And inevitably in the direction of things danger-ous, fragile, and otherwise non-baby-friendly. Every week, it seemed, the line of baby proofing rose a little bit higher. First it was outlet and power-strip covers. Then, gates were erected to keep her away from the stairs. As she started reaching higher and then pulling up to stand, knickknacks and picture frames were moved to upper shelves and cabinets were locked.

Elsa's ability to crawl and pull up coupled with her instinct to put absolutely everything into her mouth required new defen-sive strategies as well. We got in the habit of moving the cat's food—which, let's face it, looks a lot like cereal—into the (gated off) living room while we had breakfast in the kitchen and put-ting it back in the kitchen when we moved into the living room / dining room area for playtime. We always had to be on the look-out for potential hazards, always hypervigilant.

This time, we weren't worried that Clio lagged behind her sister in matters developmental; we thanked our lucky stars.

But even having one crawler and one sitter had its challenges. There was the morning when I was reading a somewhat cranky Clio one of those "touch and feel" books full of fluffy chicks (fluff matted in spots with with dried, spilled milk) and velvety horses (ditto) while Elsa slalomed happily back and forth around the legs of the dining room table a few yards away, probably eating fallen Cheerios and God knows what else off the floor. At some point I dashed very quickly upstairs—the room was baby-proofed, so I figured the girls would be OK—to find some additional textured baby books and grab a few diapers for the downstairs changing station while I was at it.

When I got back downstairs, Clio, of course, hadn't moved. But Elsa had found her way over to the cat's dishes, which we'd forgotten to put back into the kitchen, and was shoving handfuls of the stuff into her mouth while sitting in a puddle of spilled water from the overturned water dish.

("Do we have to feed her cat food for three days in a row now, to make sure she's not allergic?" Alastair asked later when I told him what had happened.)

After extracting what cat food I could from Elsa's mouth—not that it mattered, really, but the idea of one's child eating horsemeat and fish eyeballs and whatever else is in dry cat food isn't terribly pleasant, especially when, as Alastair pointed out, we hadn't formally introduced those foods yet—I grabbed the dishes and went into the kitchen to find a towel to mop up the water. There were no dish towels in sight. And the paper towel roll was empty. Of course. So I grabbed a clump of paper napkins.

Clio, meanwhile, was making cranky, half-whining / half-yelling sounds now, annoyed that I hadn't returned with additional reading material for her.

"I'm coming, Clio bear!" I called cheerily, through clenched teeth. "I've just got a situ*ation* to deal with here, OK?"

Thoughtlessly, she kept on whining.

By the time I got back, Elsa had somehow managed to get herself all the way over to the other side of the room. What followed was like one of those slow-motion movie scenes: I saw her pulling up to the coffee table; I spotted my coffee cup, which I'd neglected to move before my original trip out of the room; and I knew that she was going to make a grab for it. I dashed across the room, shouting "noooooooooooooooo!!!!" (slow-mo), but I wasn't quick enough.

Fortunately—very fortunately—the coffee that Elsa spilled all over herself was only lukewarm.

To this day, I do not put beverages on the coffee table or side tables when my children, or any other children, for that matter, are in the room. And I instinctively go around moving cups and glasses away from table edges in other people's homes, whether or not there are children there. I'm loads of fun at cocktail parties.

Once Clio started crawling, at around ten months, we got our first taste of the frantic juggling act that would be the next two and a half years and beyond. While you go after one baby, the other one is crawling in the other direction. You get one baby into a confined area or apparatus—an exer-saucer or a swing or just up onto your hip—and suddenly you're asking, "Hey, where's the other baby?" (And these may be the exact words you use, because it's entirely possible that you've lost track of which one you've got.) If you're not in a baby-proofed setting, he or she will inevitably be somewhere he or she shouldn't—a staircase, a kitchen cabinet, the edge of a cliff.

You start feeling like a combat soldier, looking for danger on all sides. You become a half-amputee octopus, learning to scoop a baby up with one arm, a diaper bag with the other, while simultaneously blocking the movement of the other baby with one leg while you kick a singing plastic toy out of your way with the other—probably with a little more force than necessary, because, good Lord, if you hear that annoying voice one more time you're going to lose your shit. Who are these women who do the voices for these toys anyway? Why do they have to sing like that, with so much warble and smile and saccharine?

This ambidextrousness extends to other activities as well, of course. By this time you've most likely already mastered giving a bottle to or nursing both babies at once. Now, you have to learn the art of simultaneous solid-food feeding. At a good meal you can get away with one bowl and alternating spoonfuls—one for Baby A, one for Baby B, one for Baby A, and so on. If it's one of those times when you've missed the ideal feeding window and they're so hungry and cranky once you've got their food ready that, in typical illogical baby fashion, they begin crying as soon as you start feeding them, you'll probably have to do the simultaneous spoon-in-each-hand approach.

You become a machine. The right hand knows not what the left is doing and vice versa. Or maybe, more accurately, your right hand knows exactly what your left is doing and the mental energy required begins to fry your brain circuits a little bit.

And once they start walking—our girls did at just over twelve months, within days of each other—everything ramps up yet again. Now you've got two upright babies who can move at a fairly good clip yet who have absolutely no sense of self-preservation. Outside the confines of your home, you will almost always need someone else with you, to play man-on-baby defense. You will understand the merit of baby "leashes," may get a pair yourself (we didn't, but we probably should have), and will never judge anyone who uses them, ever again.

You will probably be getting more sleep at this point, but you will be more physically exhausted. On the upside, as a result of all the chasing and scrambling you're doing, you'll most likely lose a few pounds.

But enough about you.

Let's talk about my boobs. Which I was still employing several times a day as the girls neared their first birthday. By now they'd lost some of their porn-star buoyancy—in fact, they'd taken on a squishy sort of feel that I realized, with some sadness, was to be their new texture. Gone the perkiness of youth.

I was still producing a good amount of milk, though I pumped less frequently and we used formula more often. Meanwhile, the girls were steadily expanding their solid-food repertoire, and showed a particular fondness for carbs (Cheerios, graham crackers, and bread—all perennial favorites) and bananas. Constipation, anyone?

Elsa was an especially enthusiastic eater. We have a fabulous picture of her at my parents' house that Christmas: she is wearing a lovely, embroidered white blouse and a crown of glittery star-studded string from the wrapping of some present. Her cheeks are rosy and cherubic, and the lights of the tree glow softly behind her as she stands at the coffee table, about to shove a fistful of crackers into her open mouth.

Elsa was also much more enthusiastic when it came to nursing during those last months. Clio seemed like she could take it or leave it. It was as if she realized it was important to me for some reason, so she went along with it. But she'd be just as happy to cuddle on my lap with a bottle or a sippy cup, thanks. The second she'd taken all the boob she could bear, she'd crawl off to find something else to do or simply to sit and smile and jabber and twinkle her little eyes at me from a few feet away while I nursed Elsa. Elsa, meanwhile, might hang out for five, ten minutes, not so much nursing as employing me as a comfy, full-body pacifier, lounging in my lap with a small warm hand on my breast. And I was happy to let her linger.

When the girls were around eleven months old, Clio went through a brief biting phase. The first time it happened was at the end of a nursing session. Clio had started getting distracted and silly and was just sort of messing around when all of a sudden: chomp! She seemed to think it was pretty funny, and I couldn't help laughing either—that is, after I yelped and said a firm "no" the way I read somewhere that you're supposed to.

I hoped it was just a fluke. But over the next couple of weeks it happened a few times out of nowhere, right in the middle of nursing sessions. And nobody was happy about it. Once, while I was nursing both of the girls at the same time, Clio bit down hard, I screamed, and both girls looked up at me, then pouted and started crying in a low, pitiful "why mommy, why?" sort of way that nearly broke my heart.

Once again, I found myself thinking about whether I should wean Clio but not Elsa. The prospect didn't seem quite as unappealing now as it had when they were just a few months old. But maybe it was time to wean them *both*. I did feel like in some ways I was holding on to breast-feeding more for my benefit than theirs. I liked the convenience of it, I liked the intimacy of it, and I liked the simple *baby*ness of it.

The girls *were* still babies, of course. But they were starting to do distinctly non-baby-like things. Like standing upright (while holding on to something) and making their first stabs at verbal communication—Elsa had started referring to dogs and other four-legged creatures as "dah!"—and even rocking and bobbing in rhythm to music. I knew it was only a matter of weeks before they'd be walking. My babies were going to be toddlers soon. And like most mothers faced with this impending change, I was a little sad. The feeling was intensified by my knowledge that, in all likelihood, we weren't going to have another baby. I'd never hold an infant of my own in my arms again. And when I stopped nursing, that would be it. I'd never again have that strange, sweet experience.

Clio's biting stopped, and I continued to nurse the girls, usually just first thing in the morning and right before bed, with the occasional "snack." Right around their first birthday we introduced cow's milk, which they immediately took to. By the time they were a year old, they were only nursing for a minute or two at each session. It was becoming increasingly clear to me that they probably wouldn't miss it if I stopped entirely.

But still, I held on.

A few weeks after they turned one, they started walking—first Elsa, and then, less than two weeks later, Clio. They'd been practicing intently in the preceding weeks. They took turns pushing each other around on the little Disney-rific riding/walking toy my parents had given them for Christmas. And they adored their music table, where they could stand and make all manner of annoying sounds issue forth while lights blinked and that damned toy voice-over woman sang watered-down scat. Elsa became proficient at scooting around the coffee table, gathering up board books, and then standing with them, unsupported, for a few seconds before plopping down into her bouncy seat for a good read. Clio still generally preferred to enjoy the action from ground level but delighted in walking while holding my hands, beaming at me the whole time.

Then, suddenly, they started letting go of tables and toys and hands.

And I started to feel ready to let go, too.

There was something else that I think contributed to my readiness to wean.

While my girls were hurtling toward toddlerhood, I was hurtling toward the end of the novel I was writing. I could taste the end of this thing I'd been working on for the past two years, and I was excited. The endorphins were kicking in, like they did toward the end of a good run. Meanwhile, I was in the midst of an especially tedious project at work, a giant, unwieldy Web site for a pharmaceutical company, which only fueled my drive to finish the novel. Working on my book a couple of hours here, an hour there, I was released from the banality of "proven in clinical trials" and "minimal adverse side effects" and endless legal copy and footnotes to hedge every claim. I was inside the fictional world I'd created, steaming ahead toward the glorious finish. I felt kind of like a superhero: mild-mannered copywriter by day, literary superstar by night.

And someday—maybe soon, if my book sold—I could flip the equation. I'd be a writer who did copywriting on the side, instead of the reverse.

I was pumped. Maybe too pumped.

Also on the horizon was my first trip away from the babies: I would be going down to New York for four days, to the Associated Writing Programs (AWP) conference: a smorgasbord of author readings and panels on publishing, craft, and teaching creative writing. Plus lots of time to socialize and schmooze and soak up all kinds of good writing energy and inspiration. It would be the first opportunity since my trip to Vermont when I was pregnant to immerse myself in a writing community and focus purely on that part of my identity for a little while.

I still hadn't quite managed to wean the girls completely by the time the trip rolled around. Maybe it felt like too much to leave them for the first time *and* say good-bye to nursing forever. But I was down to one or two nursing sessions per day. The end was near.

I felt positively giddy as the trip approached. I knew it would be difficult to say good-bye to the girls, and to Alastair, who had recently returned from another short tour overseas. But I found myself getting that old travel thrill as I chose what clothes to pack, plotted subway routes, programmed friends' numbers into my cell, and tucked a few emergency granola bars into my suitcase. I couldn't believe how liberating it felt to drive down to my in-laws' house outside the city on that cold, clear February afternoon, just me and a stack of CDs in the car. No crying or whining. No acrobatic maneuvers to retrieve lost bottles and pacifiers. When I arrived, I simply got out of the car, went inside, and had a glass of wine. No babies to carry. No changing, no feeding, no lugging bags and bags of gear. Just self-sufficient, self-contained little me again: one suitcase, one purse, one laptop (and, OK, one breast pump). It was a little like reuniting with an old friend: Jane before she was Mama Jane. I remember her! That girl was all right.

And still, when my in-laws took me out to dinner that night, I kept looking over and smiling at the one baby in the place. When I got back to the house, I started looking at pictures of the girls on my computer, then called Alastair and told him to kiss them (and himself) for me, repeatedly.

But I was still thrilled to have four days ahead to focus purely on me. And I was determined not to feel guilty about enjoying it. I could relish the time fully *and* still miss my family dearly.

And boy, did I relish.

Everything in New York sparkled. The lights, the wine, the conversation.

There's an almost electrical charge you feel when you're surrounded by people who share your passion. If you're feeling insecure or competitive or otherwise lousy, that charge can take on a negative quality. But if you're in a good psychological place, as I was, and you don't have any particular agenda other than learning and connecting and being inspired, then it's positive energy. It hums and throbs and sings.

The first day, after checking into the Hilton, where the conference was being held, and where I was sharing a room with my beautiful poet friend, Morgan, I wandered through the various exhibit halls—books, everywhere, books!—and popped into a couple of panel discussions. I saw a few classmates of mine from the Iowa Writers' Workshop, as well as people I knew from the Boston literary scene.

That evening, I met my agent for drinks and tapas and told her how close I was to being finished with my novel and how good I felt about it. She was excited; I was excited. We toasted to my future success. Then she took me to a reading by one of her clients who had just released a book and to the launch party afterward, upstairs at a strange old pub in the West Village with crooked wooden floors and nautical decor. It was full of sharply dressed, rather aloof and pretentious people, but I didn't care. The drinks were free, the appetizers were delicious, and instead of changing poopy diapers and mushing up bananas, I was in New York, at a book party. What wasn't to love?

Over the next three days, I immersed myself in all things writing-related. I also strolled through Midtown and spent a delicious two hours at the Museum of Modern Art. I met up with a couple of friends over drinks. I talked lots of shop. I felt hopeful about my writing future. Just a few more chapters, and I'd be ready to launch my novel into the open arms of the publishing world. And after that, who knew?

Still, when it was time to leave, I was ready. Driving back up to Boston I felt like I was tracing behind me a figurative line, connecting my independent, career-minded self with my mother self. Both were beautiful and both were vital to who I was.

When I arrived home, my father-in-law, who'd been visiting, giving Alastair a hand, brought Elsa to the door in his arms (Clio was in the midst of a diaper change). She looked bigger and more strawberry-blond than I remembered her. Which sounds ridiculous. Four nights away, and I forgot what my daughter looked like? But it was, after all, the first time since they were born that I'd gone longer than nine or ten hours without seeing them.

The first thing Elsa did when she saw me was make a little clucking noise with her tongue. She'd figured out how to do this just before I left: one afternoon I'd been sitting with her, making funny noises, among them clucking my tongue. She had studied my mouth intently as I did it, and reached out to touch my lips and teeth, to try to see what, exactly, was going on here. It was only a couple of days and some concerted practice before she figured out how to do it herself.

So now, she was greeting me with our special sound. It wasn't exactly the big-smile-and-outstretched-arms greeting I'd expected, but it was just as sweet. I took Elsa into my arms, and we clucked at each other as I carried her inside.

It was good to be home.

10

Shortly after I got home from New York, I bit the bullet and put the kibosh on breast-feeding. I felt ready. The girls seemed ready, too. Their love for cow's milk, Cheerios, and bananas was so consuming at this point that I doubted they'd even miss it.

So one night, I just put them to bed without nursing them first. They didn't grab at my boobs or lift up my shirt while whimpering pitifully. I think I might have folded if they had. In fact, I was slightly disappointed that they didn't.

I pumped a little, just to make sure I didn't get engorged. Same deal the next couple of days: nursing in the morning only. And then I stopped that, too.

It was all going smoothly enough, and I was still very sure that I was doing the right thing at the right time, both for them and for me. But while the transition was happening, something else was happening, too. My mood was steadily slipping.

The darkness crept in slowly, insidiously. First I started to feel slightly cranky and irritable. Little things annoyed me intensely that wouldn't have normally: a bureau drawer being stuck or one of the girls wiggling and writhing while I tried to change her diaper. (Will you stay STILL, please?) I became short-tempered, prone to snapping at Alastair and the girls.

Then I began having trouble concentrating at work. I couldn't focus—didn't *want* to focus. I had no desire to work on my novel, either. It was crap, anyway. Hokey and obvious. My Iowa classmates would have scoffed.

And I was tired. More tired than usual.

Within a few days of total weaning, I was unequivocally, unmistakably depressed.

And—this can't be emphasized enough—I don't mean "depressed" in the way that people often toss the term around. I was not unhappy about weaning—at least not consciously. Sure, it made me a little sad and nostalgic. I suppose you could say I felt somewhat wistful about it. But I didn't have any desire to backpedal and start nursing again, which I certainly could have done. It had only been a few days, and I'm sure my milk ducts would have re-upped if called upon.

I was depressed as in I didn't feel like doing anything. Nothing gave me pleasure. (The official medical term for this is anhedonia, which I've always found darkly funny for its etymological link with "hedonism." Perhaps someone should open an all-inclusive resort in Jamaica, down the beach from Hedonism, just for depressives: *Come to Anhedonia! The food is terrible, the pool is dirty, and none of the rooms have ocean views. But what do you care?*)

Meanwhile, everything felt like an enormous effort—even just getting a coherent sentence out. It was as if my brain was full of viscous, tarry muck that my thoughts and words had to struggle to wade through.

Almost as bad as the depression itself, though, was my anger and dismay at *being* depressed. How was I supposed to handle this, as a working mother of fourteen-month-old twins who had *shit to do*? This wasn't like being twenty-three, twenty-five, when, certainly, being depressed was no fun, but when my only real responsibilities were getting myself to work and taking the recycling out. Back then, I could afford the time to sit on the couch and channel surf, sleep twelve hours a day, or take long, slow, gloomy walks. I wasn't needed then. Not in the way I was now, by my children. By my husband.

But life went on, as it has a habit of doing, and I muddled through it as best I could. I wasn't so low that I couldn't get myself out of bed in the morning. I could tend to the girls' daily needs and go to work and do what I needed to do there (if not in a terribly inspired or efficient fashion). I could even manage to get dinner on the table some nights. Other nights Alastair cooked, or we ordered in.

Meanwhile, almost as if they *knew* that their mama could sorely use some extra sleep and lounging-around-feeling-sorry-for-herself time, the girls decided to take the opportunity to stop napping in the morning. Cruel, cruel babies. The morning nap was generally the longer and more predictable of the two they took at that point, and it was early enough in the morning that Alastair and I sometimes used the time to get back into bed for some extra shut-eye. But it was no longer to be.

Not quite as cruelly but just as suddenly, Elsa started freaking out about taking baths. This was completely perplexing. She'd always loved taking baths. Or as Woody Allen might say, she more than loved it. She lurrvved it. She would get all excited when she heard the water running and, once in the tub, would splash and laugh and generally have a good time, playing with bath toys, giggling with Clio, letting me make shampoo horns in her hair. But suddenly, when we tried to bathe her, she was miserable. Not just whining or complaining, but screaming, standing up, and putting her arms around us, desperate to get out. This, of course, would set Clio off, and she'd start screaming, too. Two screaming toddlers when you're feeling peachy keen is bad enough. When you're depressed, it's excruciating.

We had no idea what was going on with Elsa. The water wasn't any colder or hotter than usual, nor was the room temperature. She didn't have a diaper rash or cuts or anything that might be irritated by the water, and she hadn't had any past, traumatic experiences in the tub as far as we knew. We tried everything, from letting her bring her ga-ga into the tub with her to singing to skipping the bath altogether and going with sponge baths (also not a hit). But days when her hair was crusty with banana and oatmeal and yogurt and God knows what else— because Elsa has always liked to consume her food not just with her mouth but with her entire head—we had to grit our teeth and put her in the tub, doing our best to ignore her screams and our guilt over the fact that we were apparently torturing our own child. Washing her hair was a two-person job: one to prevent her from climbing out of the tub and the other to administer water, shampoo, etc.

It wasn't fun for anyone.

And then, almost as quickly as they had arrived, the bath terrors and nap strike vanished. Elsa was happy as a duck in water again and both of the girls were back to taking a nap, albeit a shorter one, in the mornings.

Perhaps they'd been going through their own little adjustment to weaning. And now, they were back on track.

. . .

I wish I could have said the same for myself.

And still, I didn't call my psychiatrist. I'd had depressive spells before that had lasted for a couple of weeks and then went away on their own. I thought that maybe once my hormones recalibrated themselves to my new, nonlactating state I would feel better.

But then came the day when I realized that I needed help. I got up with the girls, per usual, and trudged through the morning routine: diapers, clothes, breakfast, post-breakfast scraping of bananas and yogurt off the floor. Normally at this point I would have played with them or read them some books or set them up with some blocks or balls or whatever else was the popular toy du jour. I would be there to break up intra-sibling warfare and help them when they got frustrated or stuck with whatever they were doing. I would lunge to intervene when they were about to put themselves or our furniture in jeopardy. But that day I simply couldn't summon the will or energy to do any of this. My veins, it seemed, ran with dread. Just *being* hurt.

I gathered the girls up onto the couch with me and turned on a prerecorded episode of *Sesame Street*, praying that their attention span for TV would stretch beyond its usual ten to fifteen minutes. If I had that time, maybe, I thought, I could collect myself and summon the strength to get through the morning.

But I couldn't. Even this, even just sitting, half-reclined, on the couch, in my pajamas, was beyond me. All I wanted—all I could imagine doing—was to be back in bed, preferably asleep.

I went upstairs, where Alastair was still sleeping, and gently woke him.

"Baby," I said, "I'm sorry, but I need to go back to bed. Can you go down with the girls?"

He propped himself up onto his elbow, confused, concerned. "Are you sick?"

"No." I was on the verge of tears now. "I'm just too low."

"Why don't you just turn on the TV," he said gently. He was tired, and this was his day to sleep in. I didn't blame him for being disappointed, and I didn't blame him for not fully understanding how I could feel so awful that even a routine morning at home was unbearable.

"I did," I said. "They're watching *Sesame Street*. But I just can't be there. I'm sorry." My voice grew tight and I crawled onto bed, curling myself into a fetal position at his feet. How pathetically predictable, I thought, as my body was forming itself into this shape—this universal shape of despair—and yet I couldn't imagine stretching out on my back or my stomach. The pain pinched me inward. "I'm sorry," I said again.

"It's OK," he said, getting out of bed.

When he came back from the bathroom after brushing his teeth, he sat next to me and put his arm around my middle. "Have you called your doctor yet?" He'd been after me to do it right from the start.

"I will," I told him.

"Call her today." He bent close and kissed my cheek. "You *are* going to feel better."

"OK," I said. I felt like a child. I wanted to be a child. To have someone else take care of me. "I'm sorry."

"Don't be sorry," he said. "Call your doctor, and get better."

I woke up the day of my appointment feeling better than I had in the previous days, which happens pretty much anytime I make an appointment to see a mental health professional. Rationally,

I know it's probably because I feel a sense of relief in knowing that I'm close to getting some help, and it gives me a little mood bump. More neurotically, it makes me wonder if my symptoms really are all in my head and I'm being a wimp and faker and hypochondriac by seeking pharmaceutical help. And then I get into the appointment and the doctor asks me how I'm doing, and all of a sudden, I'm a blubbering mess.

My psychiatrist at the time was a soft-spoken, bookishly pretty woman with a rosy-hued office resembling not so much a therapy room as an Edwardian parlor. I hadn't seen her since the first time I met her, when I was pregnant and assembling my postpartum depression prevention team. Once I appeared to be in the clear for that, I frankly didn't know if I'd ever see her again. My primary care physician was happy to keep prescribing my Prozac for me "as long as I was stable."

But here I was, back in the rosy parlor, feeling far from stable. I told the doctor how I was feeling, and she nodded, with a wrinkle of sympathy above her glasses. She asked me the usual questions about my symptoms, in the usual terms psychiatrists use: Do you have trouble enjoying things you normally enjoy? (Like, for example, life? Yes.) Are you sleeping more or less than usual? (As much more as one can with twin toddlers.) How is your sex drive? (Vat eez thees "sex drive" of which you speak?)

I told her about my own quirky "bonus" depression symptoms as well—the ones that are apparently not typical, because they tend to make doctors cock their heads and look at me funny: my eyes get dry and itchy and I feel a frequent need to sigh heavily.

I also asked her if it was possible that this episode was due to the hormonal shift of weaning.

"It's not something I've really seen or read about before," she said. "But it's certainly possible. There's a lot we just don't know about the causes of depression. But," she reminded me, "it's also a big deal to stop nursing. You shouldn't discount that, or not let yourself mourn."

"I know," I said. This had, of course, occurred to me. "But I really am OK with my decision. I don't think that's what's making me feel like this."

"The weaning may not be why you're feeling this depressed now," she continued. "But it's possible that it triggered it."

I considered this for a moment. I'd never experienced a "triggering event" for my depression before. In the past, it had always just dropped in from out of the blue, absurdly irrelevant to what was happening in my life. Conversely, trying times and difficult events had never sent me into a tailspin. But maybe something in my chemistry or my psychology had changed as a result of juicing myself with hormones or getting knocked up or nursing two hungry babies for over a year.

I hoped—and assumed—it hadn't.

I left my visit with a prescription for a ten-milligram bump-up of my Prozac. The relief wouldn't be instant, I knew that; it would take a week or two, maybe more, to start feeling the effects of the increased dosage. And maybe even then it wouldn't be enough. Still, as I descended the old, narrow wooden stairs from her office, I could almost hear the gears groaning above me, preparing to lift the weight from my shoulders.

II

I told myself, when I was pregnant, that I was going to make every effort to have an individual relationship with each of my children. I was determined to regularly carve out one-on-one time with each of them, although I suspected it would be difficult. I didn't want to see them as a unit, and I didn't want them to feel like they were part of one. (Along similar lines, we've never referred to them as "the twins," which has always sounded weirdly dehumanizing to me. It's always "the girls" or "the kids.")

It was actually easiest to get one-on-one time with the girls when they were infants, and I could nurse or hold them one at a time with some frequency. But as they got older and more mobile, it became more difficult. Moreover, as my presence—the presence of my breasts, more specifically—became less essential, Alastair and I got into the habit of tag-teaming. While one of us was with the girls, the other would use the opportunity to work or write or run errands or any of a long list of other things we couldn't do while saddled with two babies, or even one.

To this day, we typically stick to this pattern of all-or-nothing child care. It's hard not to. And yet every time we do divide and conquer—one parent, one child—we say, afterward, that we really ought to do this more. It really is nice. And important.

The first time I spent extended quality time with one of the girls was when they were just shy of fifteen months old. I was still fogged in. That is, my recharged antidepressant dose hadn't yet kicked in and I was still a sedated and slightly befuddled version of myself.

It was a Saturday morning and we'd been planning to go to a kid-friendly restaurant in Cambridge that supposedly had a nice play area and a good, reasonably priced brunch. But Clio woke up with a runny nose and a fever, and it was quite clear that she was in no shape to go anywhere. Least of all a crowded restaurant full of other babies and kids.

I was so disappointed. I had really wanted to get out of the house, out of myself, and do something. (Which was a good indication that I must have been starting to feel better, because otherwise I would have been relieved at an excuse to stay home.) Alastair didn't mind so much; he was on the brink of a cold himself. But he saw that I was frustrated and flustered by this change in our plans (proof that perhaps I wasn't starting to feel better at all . . .) and suggested that Elsa and I go.

"But I don't want to go alone," I said, on the brink of tears. (No, definitely not feeling better yet.)

"You won't be alone," he said. "You'll be with Elsa."

"That's true," I said, a little bemused, and a little ashamed of myself. Because she did, of course, count as someone, didn't she?

Elsa, meanwhile, as if to prove the very point her father had just made, had toddled into the front hall and gotten her coat, which she held up to me, saying—using the universal Elsa-ese

phrase for "I am hungry, and I'd love to go out for a meal"—
"Banana! Banana!" Or, as she pronounced it, "Nana! Nana!"

And so it was that Elsa and I had our first date.

The best way I can describe the experience is to liken it to a
hide-a-key rock—the kind made of plastic, molded and painted
to look exactly like a rock. So if you bend down to pick it up,
unaware of its non-rock nature, you feel momentarily confused
and knocked off balance because it is so completely, unexpectedly light.

Which is to say that with just one child, everything was incredibly easy.

One child to put into the car. One child to take out. No
stroller. One sippy cup. Once we got to our table, Elsa sat in her
high chair across from me and played with the plastic toys the
waitress brought in a bucket to our table. (It was an *extremely* kid-
friendly restaurant.) She was very busy, and very happy.

I, on the other hand, was completely disoriented. Granted, this
was in part because my mind wasn't quite firing on all cylinders.
My entire *life* felt slightly disorienting at that point. But being
alone in a restaurant with one baby, my baby, was like nothing I'd
ever experienced before. What was I supposed to do? Talk to
her? Play with the toys with her? Should I just sit there and look
around at other people? Should I have brought a magazine?

Without Alastair to talk to or another baby to toggle my attention between, I felt a strange sense of quiet and calm, despite
the general noise and bustle of my surroundings.

After I ordered ("I'll have the blueberry pancakes and the
little lady here will have, um, some of my pancakes"), we checked
out the play area, where there was a train table and a toy kitchen
fully stocked with pots and pans and disturbingly appetizing-

looking pretend foodstuffs. Plus a variety of naked dolls and plastic animals and wooden puzzles, all happily comingling.

Here again, I was somewhat stymied. Elsa was happy to explore on her own, picking up and putting down various toys. I sort of just stood there and watched her, not knowing if I was supposed to be interacting with her or watching while looking vaguely amused or what.

I realize that this makes me sound like an idiot. And believe me, I felt like an idiot, too. I couldn't help wondering what the other parents were thinking as they watched me: Was I her aunt or a family friend, and therefore unused to this situation? Had I had too many mimosas?

If Clio had been there, she and Elsa would probably have been fighting over a naked doll or piece of plastic bacon, and I would have had to make peace between them and try to distract one or both of them with some other toy. It was also quite likely that Clio would have been sticking close by my side or even wanting me to hold her. This would have occupied 80 percent of my attention. So if Elsa had tried to go off exploring in the direction of the ladies room, as she did several times that day, I wouldn't have been able to intercept her and guide her back toward the train table. More likely, I wouldn't have known how far she'd gotten until I heard the shriek of some poor person who'd been walked in on with their pants around their ankles, and I'd have to sprint over—away from a whining Clio—to retrieve Elsa and apologize.

But I didn't have to do any of that. All I had to do was sit and watch and smile and occasionally reroute Elsa when she started heading boldly off toward the bathrooms or toward other diners' tables, or gently interfere when she innocently swiped toys away from indignant three- and four-year-olds. When our food showed up, Elsa sat across from me like a little grown-up, albeit one in a high chair, and we shared pancakes and chunks of melon and played peek-a-boo. She only once flung her sippy cup to the floor intentionally. Otherwise, she was quite well behaved. As I watched her eat—shoveling handfuls of food into her mouth and managing to cover her entire face with blueberry residue in the process—I found myself musing, in a way I rarely stopped to do when I was with both of the girls: Who was she, this little person? Who would she become? And what would our relationship be like down the road, when she had thoughts and ideas she could verbalize?

I also found myself feeling wistful about the fact that I so rarely had this chance to focus exclusively on her. Even now, my thoughts inevitably went to Clio: Was it bad that I was spending this time with Elsa? Did the fact that I admired Elsa's spunk and independence mean that, in fact, I didn't like Clio as much, on account of her cautiousness? Or, on the other hand, did it mean that Elsa and I would never be as close because I was too quick to assume that she didn't need me?

Further complicating this was my frustration at the fact that my depression didn't seem to be budging. The fog was still there in my brain, thinning perhaps, but still there, dulling all the edges and angles. I wished I could part it with my hands or blow it away, to find everything suddenly crystalline. There was my beautiful daughter, right there in front of me, and I couldn't quite see her.

At least that's what it felt like. The irony is that, in retrospect, I realize I wasn't actually as absent as I feared. I remember my brunch date with Elsa, and my thoughts and emotions during it, quite clearly. I just perceived myself to be in a more altered state than I was. Such is the malevolent mischief of depression: it makes you a stranger in your own mind.

Once we'd finished our meal, I was tempted to take off with Elsa and go somewhere else, to continue our little one-on-one adventure. A mall with an indoor play area, perhaps, or the library. Places that I hadn't yet attempted on my own with both of the girls since they'd started walking. Hell, maybe we could go get our nails done. But Alastair and Clio were waiting for us, and so we headed back home.

Clio had livened up a bit by then and was sitting on the floor playing when we arrived. I scooped her up and kissed her, hoping she hadn't felt betrayed. "We missed you, little bear!" I said. Which was completely true, even though it had been completely lovely to be alone with Elsa.

This has been the constant paradox for me in parenting twins, since the beginning and extending to the present. When I am alone with or focused on one, the other is always there in the periphery of my mind, exerting her gentle, constant pull on my heart, like a small moon.

If the girls noticed that I was less animated, energetic, or engaged than usual during this period of depression, they didn't show it. Then, they were only fifteen months old. And I did try. I tried so hard to stay present—to cuddle and play and read with them. To smile. Fortunately, being with them was one of the few things that could actually make me forget my depression for a while and feel some pale shadow of happiness.

Their verbal and nonverbal communication skills were starting to ramp up, which was exciting to witness. Elsa could say "ba" for bath; the aforementioned "nana," meaning banana and/or

food in general; and "shizz" for shoes, as well as a bevy of animal sounds: moo, baa, woof-woof-woof. (Why do we spend so
much time teaching babies to make domesticated animal sounds?
Do other cultures do it, too? Do kids in Southeast Asia go
around imitating water buffalo?)

Clio wasn't making as much progress on the oral communication front, but she was totally rocking the sign language and
the listening comprehension. She knew the signs for "eat" and
"more." And if either Alastair or I happened to say the words
"breakfast," "lunch," "dinner," or "snack," Clio would start vigorously making the "eat" or "more" signs. She also knew the
signs for cup, milk, and—usefully—monkey.

We were working very hard on getting both of the girls to
understand the sign for "wait." As in, please, you're just going to
have to wait. I know you want more banana, as evidenced by
your frantic gesticulations and persistent grunting and whining,
and I am peeling it and cutting it into small, bite-sized chunks as
fast I possibly can, but I can't do it instantly, so could you please
stop making noises like a baby cave person and try to be a little
more patient? Is that so hard?

They never really grasped "wait."

They also didn't understand "Mommy's sad" or "Mommy's
tired" or "Mommy really, really needs to just lie here on the
couch for a while and zone out, so could you guys just, like, stop
needing things?"

Still, in the context of my depression, the intensity of parenting twin toddlers was both my greatest challenge and, in a way,
my salvation.

Depression feeds on inactivity. It foments in an unoccupied
mind. The effect is cyclical: the more depressed you get, the less
you want to or can do. Which, in turn, makes you more depressed,

and so on. But with a pair of toddlers—not to mention a job and a blog I was contractually obligated to write—I didn't have the option of sitting around and brooding (or sleeping).

That is, I was healthy and functional enough that I could refuse to give myself that option.

So, dozens of times a day, faced with wrestling the girls into their clothes or into the bath, making yet another meal, or reading yet another barnyard animal book to the girls, I had the sensation that I was standing on a dock, trying to psych myself up to jump into a very cold lake (something I abhor), only about a thousand times worse.

But I would inevitably jump (what else could I do?), and—as is the case with lakes of the nonmetaphorical variety—after the initial shock and discomfort, it wasn't that bad. I could do what needed to be done. And while I was doing it, the depression didn't hurt quite as much. I could even manage to enjoy myself sometimes.

My other salvation was my husband. Alastair understood what was going on with me on a deeply sympathetic level. He knows from his own experience that depression isn't something you can just "snap out of."

"You're sick," he would say when I started to fret about the work and writing and social obligations I was falling behind on as a result of my mood, as well as the extra parenting and household burdens I was putting on him. (Guilt: another fabulous symptom of depression.) "You need to treat yourself like you would if you had a cold or the flu. You wouldn't feel guilty about not doing all this stuff if you had a bad cold, right?"

"Right," I would say, and still feel guilty.

At the same time, he would gently urge me to do things like take the girls on a walk, go to the gym, or stay up and watch a

movie with him instead of burrowing myself into bed right after dinner. "Come on, it'll be good for you," he'd say. And if I
agreed, I'd usually get teasing, mock sincere, "atta girl!" or "that's
the spirit!" or—my favorite—"that's the way to keep your pecker
up!" And usually I would laugh.

Thank God, my brand of depression usually leaves my sense
of humor intact. It impairs my ability to *be* funny, but it still
permits me the possibility of finding *other* things funny. Alastair
could still make me laugh, and this was a great blessing, probably both to me and to him. It's not easy having a wife who isn't
interested in talking or sex or doing much of anything. There
was so little I could give him in that state; at least I could give
him laughter.

Twin toddlers, as it turns out, can be awfully damned funny,
too. Like when one of them is grabbing on to the hood of the
other one's sweater or sweatshirt and following her gleefully
around the house—a maneuver we called "hoodie skiing." Or
when they decide that Tupperware containers make really good
hats. Or when they toddle around side by side in matching snow-
suits, looking like a couple of small Stay Puft marshmallow men,
giggling madly.

As lousy as I felt, I knew that as long as I could find reasons
to laugh, I could keep on going. All hope was not lost.

Laughter is good medicine. But Prozac is even better.

Within a couple of weeks after I increased my dose, I was feeling markedly better. And then, one day, I woke up and realized
that I was back. The weight in my chest was gone, my eyes didn't
itch, and I had my normal level of energy. I was astonished—as
I always am when I recover from depression—at just how *pleasant*

the most mundane things in life felt: Eating breakfast. Getting an e-mail from a friend. Reading a book. Kissing my spouse. Meanwhile, the everyday tasks that made my stomach lurch with dread before (Laundry? How can I *possibly* do laundry?) were back to being plain old everyday tasks.

Even more telling: I wanted to write again. My novel was calling out to me, begging to be finished.

But the best part of feeling better was feeling fully engaged in the girls' lives. I wasn't suddenly The Perfect Mother. I still lost my temper sometimes. I still let them eat a lot more instant mac and cheese than was probably healthy. But I didn't feel like I was parenting from inside a very thick, somewhat scratched plexiglass cube. I could manage the intensity of parenting *à deux* with relative grace, even if it did still leave me exhausted. And I could scoop one or both of my babies up into my arms and kiss their big, juicy cheeks without finding myself on the brink of tears because I was sad about being sad. Life ceased to be a tragedy. It was just life.

For the moment, I was happy. And had no reason to believe I wouldn't stay that way.

12

It was springtime in New England now, and I was excited about the prospect of taking the girls to the playground, where, for the first time, they'd be able to do more than simply be pushed on the baby swings. They could toddle around, dig in the sand, and maybe even handle some low-grade climbing and sliding.

There is a park with a small and, thankfully, enclosed playground just a couple of blocks from our house, which is perfectly serviceable despite the fact that teenage vandals regularly decorate the equipment with spray-painted penises—admirably anatomically accurate ones, at that.

I bundled the girls in their coats and hats, loaded them into the stroller, and took them there one cool but sunny afternoon in late March, pumped up for our first "big girl" outing.

Now, I don't know if it's because I had twins and was therefore more overwhelmed than the average new mother or if it would have been the case regardless, but during the girls' infancy and toddlerhood, I frequently felt like I was a step behind when it came to certain care-and-feeding needs. Not the very basic stuff; my children were always clean and clothed and fed. Nobody was breaking out in sores. But other, smaller things. Like when we were supposed to start letting them drink water in addition to milk or switch from bottles to sippy cups or start brushing their teeth. Somehow everyone else seemed to be in on this knowledge. (Maybe they were reading books? Checking Web sites?)

And because the great majority of the girls' clothes—especially during the first couple of years—were either gifts or hand-me-downs, I often forgot about the fact that we might actually, you know, have to *buy* them certain items from time to time.

Which brings me back to the playground. When we got there, Elsa immediately toddled toward the play structures and started climbing the steps up toward the slide—a small, toddler-friendly, non-phallus-emblazed one. Clio took a few steps onto the sand; decided she did not like having a strange, bumpy, mushy floor under her feet one bit; and began crying, rooted to the spot, until I came over and rescued her.

While Elsa was exploring and Clio and I stuck to the pavement, I spotted another toddler just about the same age as the girls nearby with his mother. I noted that he wasn't wearing a hat and, in a mildly judgy sort of way, thought to myself: that child should really be wearing a hat. It's quite chilly out, and the ground is rather damp. (Please feel free to imagine this inner monologue with an arch, stuffy British accent.)

I was proud of myself for actually thinking to put the girls in hats—and, OK, not *really* that disapproving of the other mom—because there had been plenty of times when I probably should have put the girls in hats and didn't.

But just when I was feeling like I'd finally reached a new level in my parental competence, I noticed something else about the poor, neglected toddler's outfit: he was wearing shoes. As in, real shoes. Little sneakers with Velcro closures, to be specific.

Cut back to Elsa's feet as they padded through the damp sand toward the steps for another slide: on them, Robeez—those little soft-soled leather shoes that are supposed to be good for babies who are just learning how to walk and that are designed for indoor use. Pink, with pairs of red cherries on them. They were given to us in a hand-me-down box from my friend Mandy, and weren't in the greatest shape—the leather was worn thin around the toes. Clio was wearing a matching pair. Reaching down to hold one of her feet, I realized that the shoe was quite cold, and slightly damp on the sole—even from her very brief sojourn on the sand.

Shit, I thought. *I've got to get my kids some real shoes.*

I quickly scooped Elsa up and brought her and Clio over to the swings on the far side of the playground, where their inadequately shod feet could dangle a yard or so above the cold, damp ground and where, I hoped, that other, much better, more organized, and generally adept mother wouldn't see them.

The girls were actually very enthusiastic about shoes as a class of objects at the time. "Shoes" (pronounced "shizz") was one of their favorite new vocabulary words, and they liked to attempt, futilely, to put their own little Robeez on. They also had, for some reason, gotten in the habit of picking up and delivering Alastair's and my shoes to us, one at a time, like little retrievers. We weren't sure if they were trying to be helpful or if they were trying to subtly tell us that we were slobs and shouldn't leave our shizz lying around the house.

We did have one pair of "real" kids' shoes at home: pink

suede sneaker-moc-type things that my mom had found at the
L.L. Bean factory store for a few bucks. They were cute, but on
the stiff side. The first time I put them on Elsa, she tried to shake
them off her feet and cried until I took them off. The second time,
she just sat down and pulled them off herself. I tried putting them
on Clio, and that didn't work out either. After clomping stiff-
leggedly around for a few steps in them looking like a cherubic
Frankenstein's monster, she stood in the middle of the kitchen
floor like she was bolted down there and cried for me to pick her
up. When I didn't, she got down on all fours and proceeded to
crawl out of the room. She refused to go bipedal until I took the
offending clodhoppers off.

And so it was that the girls and I went on our first-ever shoe-
shopping trip. I knew that it wasn't going to be easy navigating
a shoe store with the two of them now that they weren't content
to sit in their stroller for long periods of time, but I didn't know
exactly what size their feet were, and I figured that since these
were to be their Very First Real Shoes I should probably get
their shoes fitted by some professionals.

When I was a child, getting shoes meant having my feet measured by grandfatherly men at small, dimly lit, locally owned
shoe stores. They would disappear into a back room, then reappear
with shoes that they would lace, if necessary, and then personally
put onto my feet. They'd feel for my toe with a thumb when I
stood, and discuss the fit with my mother while I walked back
and forth in front of them, per their instructions. It was an experience on par with going to the doctor—very serious and official,
administered by kindly and benevolent adults concerned with my
well-being.

I'm not sure why I thought this would have been the case at
the Stride Rite outlet at the mall. As if we'd go in there and be

instantly transported back to a suburban Main Street shoe shop, circa 1978. It was, of course, like any other shoe store you'd find in a mall: bright and neon-lit, with rows of shelves stacked with various sizes. Precious few places to actually sit down and put the shoes on. A couple of bored teenagers as sales associates.

When I asked one of them if he could measure the girls' feet, he looked momentarily puzzled, then seemed to remember that he worked in a shoe store and said he'd go look in the back for "the thingy." (Which, I happen to know, is called a Brannock Device. Shoe clerks today. I tell ya.)

I quickly scanned the prices of the various toddler-sized sneakers and sandals and Mary Janes and felt myself growing queasy at the notion of spending twenty-five dollars a pair (or more) on shoes that the girls would most likely outgrow in a few months. If it had been one pair, I might have done it. But two . . . damned twins.

When the associate came back with the thingy, we measured Elsa's feet—a process she seemed to find quite fascinating—while Clio whined to be let out of the stroller. While we measured Clio's feet—something Clio did not find fascinating or pleasant in the least—Elsa toddled happily off in her socks, saying "Shizz! Shizz!" There wasn't anyone else in the store, and it wasn't that big a place, so I wasn't too worried about her. I just glanced over my shoulder now and then to make sure she wasn't on her way out the door.

It was just as I was getting Clio's Robeez back on that I heard the first box of shoes being pulled off the shelf, its contents tumbling to the floor. And then the second. Followed by "Shizz! Shizz!"

Shit! Shit!

I picked Clio up and followed the sound of "shizz!" and crinkling tissue paper to Elsa. While I was putting shoes back into their boxes and up onto the shelves the girls toddled off on their own—in opposite directions, naturally. As I was chasing after one, then the other, cleaning up the trail of destruction they left in their wake while also attempting to steal a glance at one or two shoe styles and prices, I understood suddenly why my friend Mandy had said, "are you sure you don't want to take them, just in case?" when I haughtily turned down the pair of toddler "leashes" she offered me.

We did not buy any shoes that day. But I had the girls' sizes now. Which meant that I could look for shoes online, or at other stores, or at my twin-club tag sale. By myself.

Once, when the girls were just five or six months old, while I was walking somewhere with them in the stroller, a middle-aged twinlooker stopped to take a peek and tell me that she had twins herself. The fellow parent of twins is the kind of twinlooker I've never minded. (In fact I've become one, too.) There is a sort of unspoken solidarity among parents of twins—a desire to reassure and sympathize with one another. Only another parent of twins can *really* understand what the experience is like. We ought to have a secret handshake.

This particular MOT asked me how we were doing, and I said it was hard, but we were doing fine. It was getting easier.

"Six months is a great age," she'd said, smiling fondly down at the babies. She paused, seeming to weigh whether or not to say the next thing on her mind. But she said it: "One-and-a-half to three is the hardest part."

"You think?" I said, with skepticism. Because this didn't seem right. Weren't things supposed to get easier, not harder, over time? Wasn't the first year the hardest—the sleepless nights, the crying, the nursing? Isn't that what everyone had said?

The woman nodded, with a wan smile. "One-and-a-half to three. But after that it's just wonderful. It gets easier and easier."

I had filed this conversation away far, far back in some dusty part of my head where I wouldn't find it again, I hoped, until the girls were seventeen or so.

But it kept worming its way out and I kept hearing the woman's voice—gravely, with a Boston accent (one-and-a-HAHF)—and picturing her weary smile. (Had there been a touch of schadenfreude in it?)

Now, as the girls approached eighteen months, I found myself hearing that voice again, with increasing frequency and a growing sense of apprehension. I still hoped she wasn't right. But I was beginning to suspect that she was.

"Like herding cats" is a metaphor I would come to use with increasing frequency over the next year as the girls became steadily more sure-footed and eager to explore. What is it like to go to the zoo with twin toddlers? To the playground? A birthday party? An un-toddler-proofed house? To any house, pretty much? A big ole cat rodeo.

Being at home was by far the most relaxed scenario. The first floor of our house was almost completely childproofed, safely enclosed and partitioned with gates. Surrounded by their familiar toys and books, the girls were capable of entertaining themselves to some degree. But they also liked climbing and riding on things, which required assistance. They liked to be read to, but rarely both from the same book at the same time. They fought over toys and hurt each other by accident. They were constantly hungry.

As the weather got milder, we started taking them out into

the backyard, which was a nice change of pace. We found a small plastic play structure on Craigslist, which they quickly took to, and the yard was completely fenced in, so we didn't have to worry about them making a break for it. But being outside also meant trying to keep Elsa from eating wood chips, then running to help Clio go down the slide for the fortieth time, then rescuing Elsa when she crawled up the back porch steps and couldn't get down, then picking Clio up to look at the birdies in the tree in the neighbors' yard.

I should have had the body of a nineteen-year-old field-hockey player given the energy I burned just running after the two of them. Instead, I had a sore back, a flabby tummy, and circles under my eyes. Oh yeah, and no boobs: since I'd stopped breast-feeding, my boobs had gone down a full cup size from their perky, prepregnancy selves. Or as the saleslady at Macy's who measured me for new bras put it, with a sympathetic smile, "Sorry, hon, you're an A cup now."

But hanging out flabby, boobless, and exhausted in the yard was cake compared with actually trying to go out to, say, a playground alone with the girls. In that setting, at any given moment, it was fairly likely that I was neglecting one of my children. I was the mom at the playground that everyone hated (in my own mind, anyway): the one who was nowhere to be found while my child was eating sand or whacking someone's baby on the head with a shovel or climbing up a precarious set of steps en route to the curly slide, leaving other parents morally obligated to rescue her. But it wasn't because I was busy chatting on my cell phone or flirting with the cute dad by the swings. It was because I was chasing my other child, also eating sand, whacking someone on the head, or climbing toward certain peril (and who probably needed her nose wiped, too).

Again, I found myself feeling frequently envious of my friends with one child, for the freedom they had to be out and about in the world.

It wasn't as if we were housebound. I was clearly foolhardy enough to attempt the occasional solo excursion, and if both Alastair and I were present and could play man-on-toddler defense, things were more manageable, if not exactly relaxing.

But there were many activities we had to forgo, and many invitations we had to decline.

Even playdates were a challenge. I was fortunate enough to have several friends who had had their first child within a year of me, and now that our children were all bipedal, we attempted to get together on occasion to watch our children ignore one another and/or fight over toys while we attempted to have a coherent conversation. (Because, really, when you get down to it, playdates for very young children are really mommy dates.)

And I *wanted* to see my mom friends—to talk and commiserate and feel like a social being. But, man, I was a terrible date. If it were a real date, I'd have been the guy who shows up late, keeps looking at his BlackBerry throughout the meal, spills his wine on you, and takes off as soon as he's finished his entrée because he needs to get back home to walk the dog, leaving you to pick up the check.

I remember one playdate, with a friend whose daughter was almost exactly the same age as the girls, where I literally did not sit down the whole time. These friends had a (rather large) dog, and when he greeted us at the door, Clio practically leapt up into my arms, screaming. The dog was promptly relegated to another part of the house, but Clio refused to let me put her down for another fifteen minutes.

Elsa, meanwhile, zoomed right past the toys in the living room (and past my friend's daughter, who had toddled eagerly up to the door when we arrived, and now looked mildly confused) and into the kitchen, where she began climbing up onto one of the barstool chairs at the counter and reaching for a box of goldfish crackers she saw there. (The girl is like a food-seeking missile.)

I ran in and scooped her off the chair with one hand—the one I wasn't using to hold a still-whimpering Clio—and deposited her onto the floor back in the living room with the toys. She wasn't happy about this, having already lain eyes on a snack food. Neither was Clio, who had caught a glimpse of the goldfish crackers herself, and was now saying "Cacky! Cacky!"

My friend offered to give them some, but I demurred; the girls had actually eaten vast quantities of Cheerios and raisins in the car on their way there.

Elsa was now pulling board books off a shelf one by one, which I was about to try to put a stop to, but my friend assured me it was fine. It was only after Elsa flung one of the books across the room that I interceded.

That being done, I attempted to sit down on the couch— where my friend had already settled—but Clio would not have it. Nor would she let me put her down.

"Is she OK?" my friend asked.

"Oh, she's fine," I said. "She's just going through a clingy phase." (Six months still counted as a phase, right?) "So, how are you these days? How are things going?"

We got a few sentences into a conversation, when Elsa snatched a toy saxophone out of my friend's daughter's hands, crying ensued, and my friend and I had to do the simultaneous "You can't grab things!" and "You have to share things!" conversations that parents of toddlers know all too well.

Once that was settled, we had a few more sentences of

conversation, and then Elsa pooped. Which meant I *had* to put Clio down now, to change her sister.

You can imagine how that went.

The rest of our get-together—which probably lasted all of ninety minutes, but felt more like six hours—continued in a similar vein. And sure, my friend was distracted by her toddler's needs, too. Neither of us had expected that our girls would happily entertain themselves while we discussed books and politics. Fragmented conversations are a given when small children are present.

But at least my friend got to sit down. And maybe she—along with all my singleton mom friends—simply hid it well, but she didn't seem nearly as frazzled as I felt. I could practically hear my synapses fritzing and sparking.

I never realized, until faced with the challenge of twin toddlers, what a single-minded person I am. I'd always thought of myself as a good multitasker, but I now understand that this is only in controlled environments, and preferably quiet ones. I do not do well with chaos, and I seize up in the face of too much auditory stimulus. This is problematic when you're raising twins. Especially two very loud and spirited ones like mine.

And so I frequently left playdates feeling completely spent. It was with great relief that I stepped back onto home turf. And with any luck, it would be naptime.

I'm sorry. I'm being too negative, aren't I? I'll stop (or pause, at least). Because, as I try to remind myself whenever I'm feeling down on the whole twins thing, parenting two small children at a time, especially given my circumstances—spouse as full parenting partner, roof over my head, clean bill of health for all of us—isn't what you'd call abject human suffering.

And because, once again, for every yin there is a yang, for every twin a . . . twang?

There was much about this age, and this period in our life, that was absolutely glorious. You haven't lived until you've seen two chubby baby girls hugging each other and giggling furiously. And there is nothing quite so joy inducing as the sight of two little potbellied toddlers in bathing suits, dancing to Led Zeppelin on the radio on a warm late-spring day (while their mother dances with them, doing some kick-ass air drumming and pausing occasionally to, ahem, take a sip from a glass of really cold, crisp sauvignon blanc).

It was an unending source of wonder for me to discover how different the girls were and what sorts of things they were drawn to. Elsa loved animals: she stalked the peacocks at the Franklin Park Zoo, she got up close and personal with the chickens at a farm near my parents' house, and she took great glee in "petting" our cat. (Poor cat.) Clio liked animals, too, but of the stuffed variety. She was starting to show a great fondness for soft toys and dolls and would go through periods of attachment to one particular doll, and then another; she was a nurturer.

Both of them were silly and sweet and curious and affectionate. I had the constant urge to kiss them on the mouth, and frequently did. Not in an inappropriate, incestuous way, but in an I-love-you-so-much-and-you-are-so-precious-I-want-to-quite-literally-eat-you-up sort of way. I was head over heels for them, in a way I hadn't been before. And when they started hugging each other, or pulling my face to theirs for kisses at bedtime, good Lord, my heart was so much butter you could have put it on a stack of pancakes.

Every time I thought I couldn't fall any more deeply in love with them, I tumbled just a little bit farther.

Meanwhile, depression was in the rearview mirror, growing more distant by the day, and I felt supremely content with the balance of my life once again. Alastair and I celebrated our lucky seventh anniversary that May, and while out at dinner at our favorite restaurant we raised a glass to ourselves: we were doing this parenting thing without managing to completely lose "us" in the process. Our rigorous sleep training for the girls had served us well in this department: because the girls went to bed promptly at seven, Alastair and I had our evenings to ourselves, to recover from work and reconnect with each other. Even if that just meant eating dinner in front of the TV together.

I finished the rewrite of my novel on my thirty-fourth birthday and fired it off to my agent as well as my writing-group friends and my shrewdest and most important reader of all, Alastair. Waiting to hear back from them, not having anything to work on, felt kind of like being on school vacation—no homework to do. I enjoyed the break. And at the same time, I looked forward to diving back in.

Life was good. And although the day-to-day of twin parenting felt like it was gradually ramping up in intensity, so far the sweetness outweighed the challenges.

13

During my pregnancy and the girls' early days I was aware that there was something of a hyperparenting zeitgeist in the American subculture of which I am a part—college-educated, middle- to upper-middle-class, primarily urban-dwelling professionals. Many new parents in my demographic apparently had strong, bordering on militant, feelings about things like breastfeeding and wooden toys and television and appropriate, child-centric modes of discipline. They read parenting books on the latest theories and techniques and looked down on (and pitied the children of) parents who didn't do things quite the right way.

I became more tuned into this phenomenon when I started blogging for Babble.com. The site features essays, blogs, and articles on virtually every parenting topic—feeding, discipline, sleep, education, adoption, fertility, you name it. I began reading them from time to time, as well as similar pieces on other Web sites. Most of the points of view presented were thoughtful and measured; it was the comment threads where the fangs came out.

People ripped the authors and one another apart—from behind the shield of anonymity—falling over themselves to prove that they knew best when it came to the topic at hand. And the people who weren't doing that were pouncing on the people who were, accusing them of being judgmental. Epithets like "helicopter parent," "breast-nazi," and "sanctimommy" were flung about. Particularly dramatic commenters told one another that they were unfit parents or that they needed therapy.

And all over whether a mother let her three-year-old use a pacifier or whether a family did or didn't use "time-outs" for discipline.

I thought all of it was a load of horse poop. It seemed absurd to me that people should spend so much mental energy fretting about this stuff. Our parents, for the most part, didn't, and we all turned out more or less OK, right? And for those of us who didn't, those who had eating disorders or drug problems or spent years in therapy, well, it's probably not because our parents didn't use the right sleep-training method or carry us around in slings all day long, right?

I planned to raise my kids on instinct and common sense. Sure, I would read a parenting book or two if I needed some guidance. But I wasn't going to worry about doing everything exactly right, and I certainly wasn't going to worry about what the other mommies on the playground thought. Screw them and their sanctimommious ways!

Sometimes I'm so full of horse poop.

I tell myself (and in many cases, Alastair) these sorts of things with all kinds of pep and bravado: *I'm not going to worry about my weight anymore! There are much more important things in the world to worry about, and this is my body, and I love it! Who cares if people think I'm skinny or fat or whatever.*

I'm not going to be intimidated by my classmates at Iowa, even if they're all much, much better writers than I am. I don't care what they think and I'm definitely not going to turn into a paranoid, insecure mess!

But sadly, I do worry—far too much—about what other people think.

I've made major progress over the years. The older I get, the more comfortable I am in my own skin and the less time I spend wondering what's going through other people's heads as they look at or talk to me. I'd thought this improvement would extend to parenting as well. But, to my chagrin, it hasn't.

When the girls were teeny tiny babies, it wasn't much of an issue, since the only other mothers I had contact with were good friends. I wasn't overly concerned with their opinions on my mothering ability because apparently I care more about what complete strangers think than what my closest friends do. Which makes just loads of sense.

Now that I was spending more time in public locales, playgrounds in particular (ugh), I found myself suddenly surrounded by other parents and wondering: Wait, am I doing this right? Am I hovering too closely or letting them stray too far? (I did cut myself a little slack on this particular issue, given the twin factor.) Am I setting enough limits? Being too lax when, say, one of the girls continues to dump sand on the ground outside the sandbox after she's been told it's a no-no, or am I expecting too much of them at their age?

As the girls neared eighteen months, they were starting to develop strong opinions about things. And when reality, or my opinions, did not align with their vision of what ought to be, they got whiney and even a little defiant. They understood the meaning of "no," and we had to determine how to use that word effectively— and what to do when *they* used it. At the same time, they lacked the verbal ability to fully express or explain what they wanted, and it frustrated them. We were seeing the first stirrings of Toddlerhood with a capital T—not just the baby toddling sort—and the limit testing, pickiness, and (sigh) tantrums inherent therein.

They were also becoming clever enough to experiment and see what kind of response their actions evoked. Once, for example, Clio decided to grab on to and shake the floor lamp in our living room. Just, because, you know, it was there. It had a sturdy, weighted base, so she wasn't too likely to topple the thing, but it wasn't entirely outside the realm of possibility, and anyway I didn't particularly want her shaking this lamp, which was the single most expensive piece of lighting equipment we'd ever purchased, having cost more than $39.99. And, of course, I wanted to send the message that, generally speaking, it's not OK to shake lamps.

So I firmly told her, "No, no, Clio, don't touch. That lamp could fall and hurt you, and you could get a very bad boo-boo," etc., etc. (Somewhere I'd heard or read that it was a good idea to talk to little ones as if they understand much more English than they actually do.)

Clio apparently found this very funny. She took her hands off the lamp, smiled, and then held on again, eyes twinkling, waiting for my reaction. So I said "no" again. And what did she do? She laughed. It was at this point that a more competent parent than I might have tried to distract her with something else—a toy, a book, a piece of Tupperware. Or they might have simply scooped her up and moved her somewhere else. But I, being an idiot, and rather stubborn myself, just said "no" again. This time she let go and started to walk away, but then, grinning, went over and touched the lamp with one finger to see what I would do.

And I couldn't help it: I laughed. Thereby completely negating the effects of all the stern no-ing I'd been doing.

At this point it finally occurred to me: hey, I should try distracting her with something else! Here. Have a one-quart Rubbermaid snap-lock container. You can put some LEGOs in it and shake it. It's the greatest thing ever, trust me.

But that was a best-case scenario. Elsa was otherwise happily occupied with something, so I could devote my full attention to Clio for more than a few seconds. The more typical scenario would have been that while Clio was shaking the lamp, Elsa was standing at the baby gate in the kitchen doorway, rattling it like a problem prisoner, yelling "cah! cah!" because her toy ride-on car was over by the fridge, where she'd parked it, and she wanted desperately to get in there and go for a spin.

So instead of telling Clio to stop in a developmentally appropriate and self-esteem-promoting manner, I would be more likely to say, "No, Clio, stop it," so I could quickly go let Elsa into the kitchen. But then I'd hear the lamp being shaken ever more violently, pivot back to Clio, and scoop her up onto my hip, prompting her to start whining and screaming because, hey, she was having fun with that lamp. Then I'd go over and open the damned gate for Elsa and put Clio down, sprinting back after her when she made a beeline for the lamp again, just as Elsa started crying because she crashed her car into the kitchen table, not having quite mastered backing up yet.

Should I go on?

With increasing frequency I found myself in such scenarios as this, feeling powerless and harried and clueless, parenting from the hip instead of in any carefully considered way. In public, it was even more challenging.

And whether it was real or only in my mind, I felt the gaze of other parents on me. I felt like, in their ample free time—because they only had one kid, or one kid and a tiny baby, the lucky bastards—they must read parenting books or go to seminars or something.

I suspected I was being a bit paranoid. Maybe they were staring at me in admiration, awed by the fact that I had twin toddlers and yet still appeared to have showered within the week. I knew I should stop worrying. We were all just doing the best we could, right?

Somehow Alastair didn't worry about this stuff half as much as I did. Maybe it's a guy thing. Maybe they just don't feel the same pressure or expectation that this stuff is supposed to be instinctual for them. He had a different set of insecurities when he was at places like playgrounds and the baby gym with the girls: as a man, he felt like a bit of an outsider. He felt as if most of the moms (and by far the majority of parents out and about with their kids during the week were moms) were unfriendly and awkward toward him. They were reluctant to engage him in the casual chitchat that happens between women. (Your daughter is adorable. How old? Mine, too. Yes, they're twins. Fraternal.) He felt as if his initiating conversation with them would make them think he was sleazy, or trying to flirt.

I told him that this was all ridiculous and that, really, it was because they were intimidated by his good looks and animal sex appeal. They were afraid of the powerful attraction they might feel, which would force them to confront their disappointment and ambivalence about their own marriages.

His response to this theory was, in essence, that I was full of horse poop. But I think he secretly liked it.

By early May, the verdict was in from Alastair, my writing group, and my agent on my novel draft: it was very, very close, and with some minor revisions and polishing, it was ready to be released to the mercy of the publishing world. I was pumped up, and dove back into what I hoped would be the final draft with vigor and passion.

Never had I written so furiously or lived so completely inside a piece of writing. I have always liked the final stages of revision—the tweaking and trimming and finessing that prepare the work to meet the world. To use a birth metaphor, the worst of the labor is over, we can see the head, and all we need are a couple of final pushes and . . . voila. With luck, a professional editor will wipe the metaphorical blood and vernix and other gunk off before the baby/book is presented, swaddled in a lovely cover, to the public.

Sometimes I would find myself driving home from work in the evening so utterly absorbed in the world of the book, the questions of how to make this or that scene or epiphany work better, that I would end up turning down my street hardly aware of how I'd gotten there. I found myself working at night after the girls were in bed, staying up until midnight, with the feeling that I could have kept going into the wee hours if I didn't have the sense to stop and get some rest.

I'd never felt quite this way before—high on the creative process and the hope and anticipation of sending my baby out into the world. I felt supremely confident that this book was going to find a publisher. I was sending positive vibes out into the universe. I pushed away any doubts that bubbled up from the depths of my mind. One of my favorite professors at the Iowa Writers' Workshop, Elizabeth McCracken, told us in her novel workshop that to help us remain confident throughout the long, lonely process of writing a novel, we "must have delusions of grandeur." I most certainly did.

I was neglecting Alastair a little; I was aware of it, but he was going through an unfortunate phase of addiction to online poker (he was disciplined, at least, about the money part, putting only fifty dollars into the pot to play with and managing never to get down to zero—the stakes were low). I was wary of and slightly annoyed by this, but also too absorbed in my work to make an issue of it. I think we were both hungry for some sort of release from the growing intensity of taking care of the girls, and it fueled our respective addictions. It felt good to escape into our own little worlds, a bit removed from reality. Probably it wasn't the healthiest thing. We were lucky that it was temporary and didn't do any lasting damage. And we were fortunate that we were both able to come back and be present—mostly—when we needed to focus on the girls.

Sometimes I found myself feeling anxious, antsy, as I barreled toward the finish line. Caught up in the tangles of character and plot, I went through periods of feeling claustrophobic, trapped inside this living, breathing world that was my book. Other times, I felt almost queasy with anticipation. I was at the edge of a precipice, about to fly.

"Congratulations," my agent said after reading the final draft. "Let's go." And off it went, to a handful of carefully chosen editors at various publishing houses.

There were a few early no's. Complimentary enough: *Wonderful writing, such a confident voice. But overall, the novel felt a bit too quiet. A little too small for the books we're having success with today, in this difficult market. I'm sorry, but I just didn't fall in love.*

Frustrating, but I wasn't overly worried. And then, at last, there came some encouraging news, from one very big and reputable publishing house, and then another: *I love this. I'm passing it along to my colleagues to get their opinions.*

I was buoyed and hopeful, but not surprised. Of course. This was what was supposed to happen. And look at me: a mother of twins, with a job, a blog, a happy marriage. I was kicking ass. I was soaring.

The girls were making their own leaps forward, particularly with regard to their language skills. They constantly surprised us with new additions to their vocabularies.

One summer morning as I was getting their breakfast ready—whole-wheat frozen waffles topped with applesauce, always a big hit—Elsa exclaimed "wa-foo!"

Oblivious as always, I first just smiled and repeated, in my dopey mom voice, "Yeah, wa-foo!" and then it hit me: by George, the girl is saying waffle! How long has she known this? Has she been holding out on me? What else can she say? Pancakes? Eggs Benedict? So, of course, I started hooting "Yes! Waffles! That's right! Good girl! Waffles!" and then tried to find ways to use "waffle" logically in sentences for the rest of the day. ("Remember at breakfast when you ate a waffle?" "You look very waffle today, Elsa!" "Dinner time! We're not having waffles!")

Soon after that, maybe even the same day, the three of us were hanging out in the backyard, and Clio started pointing toward the porch and saying, "Buh buh! Buh buh!" I caught on a little quicker this time: she was pointing at a container of bubble stuff on the rail. She wanted me to blow bubbles! And so I did, until I was dizzy and had to sit down. Within a few days, Elsa started saying bubbles, too, but pronounced it slightly differently, more like "bah-boo."

I found it fascinating that two babies raised in exactly the same household, who heard each other talk all the time, had different dialects. One of the most interesting examples was the fact that Clio said "Mama" and "Dada" while Elsa said "Mommy" and "Daddy."

And it felt so completely wonderful that they were starting to call us this. Granted, they still occasionally called random strangers, mailboxes, and ducks Mommy, too, but most of the time they got it right.

It was also interesting that they didn't both have the same words. Elsa had flower ("flou") and stairs ("dee"), but Clio had baby ("bay-bees") and eyes ("ise"). I'm sure someone could have had fun coming up with a complex and ridiculous theory on the psychological significance of this, or what it suggested about the girls' future lots in life. (Clio is going to be a doctor and Elsa is going to be a landscape architect?)

At the same time as this flurry of verbal development was happening, we noticed the girls were in much better moods. The fussiness and whininess that had been steadily increasing in the prior weeks suddenly dissipated a bit.

We began to see this pattern of developmental fits and starts over and over again: a period of difficult behavior—crankiness or neediness or even just being sort of "tuned out," in their own little worlds—followed by a surge forward, when suddenly they were able to do or say or express things that they hadn't before. Sometimes the girls both went through these dark-to-light phases at the same time. Sometimes (more mercifully) they took turns. In this case, the less high-maintenance twin tended to be even more easygoing than usual. Twin yang in action.

14

In late July, Alastair went to Virginia as the musician in residence at a Unitarian Universalist family retreat and conference. I was on my own with the girls for a few days—with a little help from our sitter—and then drove down with them to my aunt's house in Connecticut, for my cousin's wedding, en route to five days' vacation at another aunt's house, on the Jersey Shore.

Traveling with two nineteen-month-olds (not to mention twenty-four month-olds, thirty-month-olds, and thirty-six-month-olds) is not for the faint of heart. Clothes, diapers, portacribs, sheets for cribs, blankets, stuffed animals, white-noise machine, brush, barrettes, shampoo, bibs, sippy cups, spoons, bowls, plates, washcloths, instant mac and cheese packets in case all else failed. (Pause for breath!) Booster seats, bathing suits, sunblock, books, toys. Multiply all of this by two, and you begin to get the idea.

Having someone look after your toddlers while you're packing, even if that "someone" is the cast of *Sesame Street,* is pretty much essential. Otherwise you might end up in the scenario I found myself in several months later, heading out on another trip while Alastair was away, packing the girls' suitcase while they "helped" by pulling every single item of clothing out of their bureau while gleefully exclaiming "Out! Out!"

Of course, there's all *your* stuff to pack, too. While I am good with packing for very long trips, i.e., backpacking through South America, where I have ample time to plan, I am a mess when it comes to packing for shorter jaunts. Seriously, as soon as I put an empty suitcase out on the bed, it's like my IQ drops fifty points. There I'll be, twenty minutes later, having packed nothing but socks, holding a pair of hiking boots in one hand and a cocktail dress in the other, muttering to myself about bobby pins.

It was fortunate that my parents were there to help us get out the door for this particular trip. And miraculous that the girls endured both the three-hour drive to Connecticut and the four-hour drive to Ocean City the next day, complete with stretches of bumper-to-bumper traffic on the Garden State Parkway, without melting down. I sat in the back, wedged between their car seats, and served as entertainer, soother, snack provider, and pacifier pop-back-in-er (we were still letting the girls use their ga-gas in the crib and the car).

Being back there with them, thanks to my parents' embarrassingly large SUV, for which I regularly used to give them shit, eliminated the need for the acrobatics I was used to performing from the front passenger seat when Alastair and I went anywhere with the girls: contorting my body into ever-more-death-defying bends and stretches to retrieve dropped toys, snacks, and pacifiers and end resultant misery. We eventually got wise to the pacifier thing and started tying them to strings around the backs of the front seats so they couldn't fall out of reach. Strangulation hazard? Perhaps. Lifesaver on car trips? Absolutely.

My aunt in Connecticut had arranged for a teenage neighbor, under her mother's close supervision, to take care of the girls while I went to my cousin's wedding with the rest of the family. After thoroughly briefing the sitters, I went upstairs to get ready. As I was zipping up my dress, feeling vainly proud of myself that it still fit, if a bit more snugly, four years after the last time I'd worn it, the phone rang.

The name that came up on the display was my agent's. My heart flipped into paroxysms: Was this it? The news I'd been waiting for? The big yes?

"Hi Jane," she said. Already I could hear in her voice what was coming: "I'm afraid I don't have good news."

Paroxysms stop. Heart plummets.

"No?"

"No. P— is passing. I'll send the note along to you. There were just too many lukewarm reads, apparently, and the executive editor wasn't enthusiastic."

She went on to say how sorry she was, how terrible she felt. Things were just so bad for the fiction market right now. It was such a wonderful book, and if it were a few years ago, she could have sold it in a matter of days.

I asked her about the other editor who'd also been interested. Had she checked in with her? Was there still interest?"

"It seems to be waning," she said.

I was ever the optimist: "There are still a few people we haven't heard back from, aren't there? And there are plenty of other publishers out there, right?"

"There are," she replied, in not a terribly convincing way. "Let's touch base on Monday, OK? Again, I am just so sorry."

As I put on my makeup and did my hair, I gave myself a pep talk in the mirror. The fact that there had been serious interest was a good sign, right? And all the complimentary, even apologetic, rejections? There was no reason to lose hope. It was a good book. A *great* book.

"Hang on to those delusions of grandeur, baby," I said to myself. I put on my lipstick, took a deep breath, and went downstairs to say good-bye to the girls. They were in the backyard, crawling through a collapsible tunnel that the sitter's mother had brought over, clearly having the time of their lives. I called good-bye to them from the screened porch, not wanting to make a big deal of my exit. The sitter tried to turn the girls' attention toward me, but they were oblivious—happily, joyfully engaged in the activity at hand.

Beautiful girls, I thought to myself. I am so utterly blessed.

Later that night, I called Alastair from the parking lot outside the wedding reception hall and told him about the news from my agent. He gave me more or less the same pep talk I'd given myself about the book, the disappointment. "Keep your pecker up," he said.

"I am," I told him. "I think I really am."

I was excited for this next leg of the vacation, looking forward to seeing my relatives—a whole different set, from the other side of the family this time—and introducing the girls to them. We'd be staying in what used to be my grandmother's house, now my aunt's, just blocks away from the beach, the ocean visible from its shaded, breezy porch on the second floor.

Alastair was there when we arrived, having driven up from Virginia that day. Seeing him felt like coming home. That night there was a big dinner, and everyone was there: my aunt, my cousins, their kids, my brother and his wife, my parents, and Alastair's parents, who'd come down for a few days. It was Familypalooza.

I prayed nobody was going to ask about my writing.

After the girls had gone to bed, Alastair and I walked down to the beach together and slipped off our shoes. The salt and suntan-oil smell of the cool sand, the creosote smell of the boardwalk pilings, drew me back to childhood and our summer visits here: endless days at the beach and cool evenings on the boardwalk—rides, Skee-Ball, caramel corn. This was the first time I'd been back to Ocean City in the four years since my grandmother's death. It was strange without her—the card games we used to play on the porch, the dinners she made—and I missed her, yet I was happy to be here, introducing the girls to this place that was so special to me.

Alastair told me about his week, which he enjoyed. Unitarian Universalists were a pretty cool bunch.

"What about you?" he asked. "You still feeling OK about the book?"

"Yeah, definitely," I said. "I mean, it's only the first round, right? There are a lot of other publishers out there. So I'm not going to let it get me down. That would be stupid."

I was working hard not to overreact or get ahead of myself. The power of positive thinking and all.

"Good," Alastair said. "It's a great book, baby. Someone's going to want to publish it."

"I know," I said, "I'm not worried."

I didn't say anything about the melancholy that I felt sneaking into the periphery of my emotions. Because wasn't it natural to feel let down after so much excitement and anticipation? Although it felt like the stirrings of depression, I told myself it couldn't possibly be. I was on the right dose of medication now. And anyway, I didn't have "triggering events." The weaning thing had been chemical, my body recalibrating and readjusting after the monumental hormonal upheaval of giving birth to and nursing two babies.

This slight—and perfectly understandable—sadness, I told myself, would certainly evaporate in the warmth of sand and sun and family.

Our first day was lovely, despite an overcast sky. We took the girls to the nearly empty beach in the morning, armed with buckets and shovels. Clio was not happy. She seemed overwhelmed by the noise and scale of the ocean, and although we got her to do a little bit of splashing in the wet sand, she was much happier back in the dry sand, helping me dig a big hole. Elsa—true to her temperament—was more adventurous, apparently intrigued by this thing the ocean. And still, a bit ambivalent: she would run down toward the water's edge in the wet sand, but if a wave rolled up too close or too fast, she'd run away in the opposite direction, yelling "no! no! no! no!" (Who among us hasn't felt the same way about the ocean at times?)

It never ceases to amaze me how different two siblings—born at the same time and raised in the same home—can be. Nature kicks nuture's ass.

And nature was about to kick my ass, too.

Later that day, during the girls' nap, when I tried to read a book, I couldn't focus on it. I even felt a mild sense of revulsion toward it: a novel. A recently published literary novel. A door smugly closed to me. I was snappy and impatient with the girls in the afternoon, annoyed with having to chase after them in the non-baby-proofed house. And in the evening when Alastair and I played Scrabble, I only lasted a few turns before I wanted to stop and go to bed. My mood was most definitely darkening.

But the sun was shining the next morning, promising a good day. I looked out the window at the wedge of pure blue sky between the houses across the street and told myself everything was going to be fine. After breakfast, I brought the girls back upstairs to get ready for the beach. But they were riled up and silly, with no interest in getting dressed. I had to physically hold them down to try to wrest their diapers and clothes onto them, and found myself quickly losing my patience. *Dammit, sweetheart, stop. Stay still. Please, stop! Will you please just stop? I can't do this! Don't you understand? I can't do this!*

When you find yourself pleading, on the verge of tears, with a nineteen-month-old, it's a sign that something probably is not right.

It felt like a gathering storm. I could almost see the clouds closing in, the menacing black-blue kind, spreading their shadow over me. Pressing down.

When Alastair came back upstairs, wondering what was taking so long, he found me sitting on the floor, my back against the bed, staring into middle space, while the girls toddled around, half-dressed, pulling the room apart—books off the shelves, clothes out of their suitcase, blankets off our bed—like little gremlins.

"What's going on?" Alastair asked. "Are you OK?"

"I can't move."

"Are you hurt?"

"No."

"You're depressed?"

"Yes."

"When did it get so bad?"

"I don't know. This morning."

"Come on," he said gently. "Try to get up. You'll feel better once you get going."

"No," I said and crawled up onto the bed. "I can't. Go ahead without me. I'll meet you guys down there."

He paused, sighed. I didn't blame him for feeling exhausted in advance at the prospect of getting the girls ready and packing up all their gear while they marauded around the house and then getting them to the beach on his own. It was a task of Herculean proportions, even when shared by two people. Which is why I knew I was utterly incapable of performing it.

But he said, bless him, "You don't have to come. It's OK. Do what you need to do."

I started to cry. Because I did feel awful about abandoning him, and terrified of how I was supposed to deal with this, this crisis, in the presence of ten thousand relatives. "I'll come," I said. "I have to. What's everyone going to think?"

Both my parents and his knew I struggled with depression, but with the exception of my father, who'd been through it himself, I never had the feeling they truly understood it. They would say, *but she seemed just fine yesterday* . . . Or, worse, they'd want to talk with me about it, ask me questions, give me advice. And what about my aunt? My cousins? I rarely saw them, and didn't particularly feel like "coming out" to them.

The irony of all this is that back in March, I had written openly about my postweaning depression on my blog. I even made a plea for other depression sufferers to be more open about their condition—both so they could get the help and support they needed, and to help remove the stigma around depression. I wrote: "I want, someday, for it to be as acceptable to say to someone 'I'm having a rough day with my depression' as it is to say, 'I think I'm coming down with a cold.' "

And here I was, afraid to tell my family what was going on. Embarrassed, ashamed, not wanting them constantly scrutinizing my behavior (*Is she better yet? Why is she smiling? Or not smiling?*) or tiptoeing around me.

"I can tell them you don't feel well," Alastair said. "But why don't I tell your parents, at least, what's going on. Your dad, anyway?"

I assented to this.

He finished dressing the girls and brought them downstairs.

When he left, I started to sob. It came and came and came, and I couldn't stop. My entire body ached from within. I felt as if my life had suddenly shrunk to the room I was in: the bed, the bookshelves, the dresser. I could not conceive of any life or any future beyond this room, right now.

And yet I knew I wouldn't ever, couldn't ever, kill myself. I would not do that to my family, or even myself. I would just stay here, in the tiny box of my being, and suffer for the rest of my life.

This was the first time I had ever felt true despair.

And I knew that what had happened was this: the real event of my disappointment over the book triggered the chemical depression. (The wine I'd had at my cousin's wedding, and at dinner the previous night, probably didn't help either.) The depression then got its claws into my disappointment and pulled me down, down, down.

I was able to force myself out of bed an hour later, feeling a little stronger if not any less ill, and take a very slow, solitary walk. By afternoon I rallied somewhat, but night was worse, and the morning was hell once again. I called my psychiatrist, and when she asked—as, it seems, mental health clinicians are always obliged to ask—if I felt I felt suicidal, I paused a beat before saying no. She phoned a prescription in to a local pharmacy—another ten milligrams tacked on to my Prozac dose.

The next two days were a little better. I could push past the morning paralysis—*onto the pier, into the lake, don't think, just jump*—and put on a good face. Being surrounded by family, in a crowded house, with two very overstimulated and overtired toddlers in the mix, I didn't have much choice. Again: duty as salvation. A bitter pill to take, but one that kept me from getting sucked down any farther than I already had.

The struggle of the week was mitigated by moments of extreme sweetness: my cousins' kids, four boys ranging in age from eight to thirteen, delighted in playing with the girls and even indulged their current addiction to ring around the rosy (or "ashy, ashy" as the girls called it).

One afternoon we brought the girls up to the boardwalk for their first-ever amusement park rides, grandparents in eager attendance. We decided that the Tin Lizzie ride would be a good start: little old-fashioned cars that went around in a circle, nothing more. Elsa, we figured, would be game, but Clio probably wouldn't.

If you want to see God laugh, my friends, pigeonhole your twins.

The minute we put her into the car, Elsa started crying and reaching up to be rescued. It was Clio who stayed on to enjoy the ride. She held on to the steering wheel for dear life, looking to be slightly in shock the whole time, sneaking only quick, sideways glances at us as we waved to her like lunatics from the side. We weren't sure if she was terrified or was having the time of her life and just being a very responsible driver. It turned out to be the latter. When it was time to get off, she cried to go back on again.

And might I suggest amusement park rides as effective, drug-free remedies for the temporary relief of some depression symptoms? My mother and I went on the Trabant—a spinning, undulating, rotating wheel. My mother cackled the whole time, which made me giggle. And then my brother and I hit the Spanish Galleon—a big ship that rocks back and forth, swinging up so high that your stomach stays aloft after you drop.

We sat in the very tip of the starboard and, at the top of the boat's arc, made very realistic puking noises, thus totally freaking out the teenage girls sitting two rows beneath us.

The trip wasn't a complete failure.

Unfortunately, it would be almost a month until I felt like myself again—until my chest stopped aching, my eyes stopped itching, and I didn't feel like a stranger in my own life and body. There would be days when I felt almost normal and days when I would have to leave work and come back home halfway through the day because I couldn't get a blessed thing done. On one particularly awful day in August I wrote in my journal:

> *It hurts, it aches, it pulls, it dulls, it weighs, it paves over any sense of drive or will or desire or hope. It puts me to bed and makes me stay there. I can act like I'm over it, for a little while. S— and E— were here today for brunch and I probably seemed almost normal. Maybe just a beat behind. But once company is gone and I'm alone, I sink.*

But gradually, the fog lifted, the sky cleared, insert metaphor of choice here. I was taking pleasure in life again, enjoying my children, my husband, my work. As for my book, well, things didn't feel quite so dire anymore, and the fact that the economy (and the publishing industry along with it) was basically collapsing beneath the nation's feet gave me, oddly, some sense of solace. It wasn't my book; it was bad timing. And anyway, there were still plenty of editors out there. If only I could get my agent to call me back.

15

During this time in their lives, the girls' relationship with each other began to truly blossom. They were playing together on their own for longer stretches of time (and by that I mean up to ten minutes), and I felt like we were—finally!—getting to enjoy this benefit of twindom that everyone had promised us would come. They were calling each other by name: "Sessa" and "Kee-o." They thought it was awfully fun to hold hands and walk that way around the house and the yard and sometimes in public, melting the hearts of onlookers. And they even, occasionally, managed to share toys without the need for parental refereeing.

Elsa thought Clio was freakin' hilarious. Clio's antics, which included pretending to be asleep in the middle of meals and doing spontaneous downward dogs on the living room rug, were a source of endless amusement to Elsa and to all of us. Miss Elsa, meanwhile, still led the way in gross motor skills activities—

climbing, digging, exploring—and Clio often followed her lead, with varying degrees of success.

Elsa was also emerging as the social ambassador of the pair, eager to loudly "hi" and "bye" anyone they encountered, while Clio generally stuck to smiles and waves. Clio's public and private personas were beginning to diverge, and would continue to do so over the next year and a half: kooky and talkative at home, hesitant and reserved elsewhere.

I never witnessed, and still haven't, any kind of "twin talk"— words or phrases that the girls used with each other that nobody else could understand. But there were times that they would be playing or even just sitting together and suddenly start cracking up for no reason I could discern.

I did notice two modes of interaction that struck me as possibly meaningful where their twin-ness was concerned. One of their favorite games, starting when they were around this age— that is, a few months shy of two—was to play in and around the long curtains in front of the sliding doors to our back porch. Specifically, one of the girls would hide behind the curtains, and the other would touch or hug or poke at her from in front. I think I might have read somewhere that twins often like this kind of thing: a reenactment of their time in the womb together, when they interacted—or simply inadvertently punched or kicked each other—between the membranes and liquid that separated them.

OK, maybe that's hooey. Maybe lots of sibling pairs like to do the curtain game. But it has still always struck me as a sort of instinctual behavior on their part, something they are drawn to doing again and again and that they seem to find particularly satisfying and fun. Humor me.

Here's another one: as I'm sure is the case with many young siblings, twin or not, Elsa and Clio have always loved roly-polying about on the floor or the ground together. Frequently, it would start as playful and then eventually, or sometimes quickly, turn ugly. There is a fine line between laughing and crying, and we got in the habit of listening, waiting for the moment the line got crossed: ten, nine, eight, seven . . . and there it is.

In the play-to-violence scenarios, it tended to be Elsa who was the perpetrator and Clio the victim. Physically speaking, Elsa has always been the "alpha twin," befitting her firstborn status, I suppose. Usually she didn't intend to hurt Clio; she was just oblivious to her own strength, and often liked to show her affection in a rather, er, passionate manner. I myself would frequently be surprised by an enthusiastic toddler Elsa coming up behind me while I was sitting on the floor or ground and throwing herself full force onto my back, wrapping her arms around my neck, and "hugging" me from behind. She's a little like Lennie in *Of Mice and Men*. She means well. Usually.

But—and here's the twin-specific part—there were also times when Clio would take the lead and basically just lie on top of Elsa, sometimes "kissing" her by way of an open mouth against her head or cheek. They'd both make sort of affectionate "mm-mmm" sounds, on the brink of laughter. Sometimes Elsa wasn't in the mood for this sort of thing, or felt trapped after too much of it, and, again, the sounds of pleasure turned to sounds of pain. But many times they'd just lie there like that for a while, and I always wondered: was this a position they found instinctually comforting because it was the way they were in the womb, Elsa on the bottom, Clio on top?

Strangely enough, during the early months of my pregnancy,

Clio had been down below and Elsa up top. At some point, around my fifth or sixth month, they switched places. I'm not sure exactly how the radiologists were able to determine this, but I took their word for it. And, given the girls' personalities, it makes complete sense. I can just imagine a little fetal Elsa, shoving her way past fetal Clio, saying, "Look down there, I think I see a light! Let me by, I want to see what's going on!" and fetal Clio saying, "Hey, sure, be my guest. I'll just hang back here and assess the situation from afar. You lead the way."

They are individuals. I try never to forget that, and I get annoyed when other people do. As the girls grew, I became increasingly careful not to describe them relative to each other: Clio is more X than Elsa. Elsa is more Y than Clio. But certainly they will become increasingly cognizant of the differences between themselves as they get older. They will inevitably, unconsciously, shape and influence each other. They will slip into patterns of reaction and interaction, some for better, some for worse.

And, inevitably, our interactions with them will have an influence, too, both on how they see themselves and how they relate to each other. Because although we absolutely love both of the girls *equally*, and try very hard to treat them equally—that is, with equal fairness and attention and affection—we can't treat them exactly the *same*. Because they aren't the same. They are two different people.

Which is also why Alastair and I had resolved, basically the moment we found out we were having twins, that we would not dress them alike. We didn't even have to resolve it, really; we both knew the other would be completely opposed to the idea.

People did give us matching outfits as gifts, and we inherited some matched sets of clothes as hand-me-downs from other parents of twins, but this wasn't problematic: we simply didn't put both girls in the same clothes at the same time. Sometimes we'd even stash the match of a shirt or pair of pants in the diaper bag, so if, say, Elsa managed to spill an entire bowl of yogurt on herself while we were at a friend's house (notice how in the spilling/sloppiness anecdotes, it's always Elsa?), we'd just take off the drenched garment and whip out a clean version from the bag. Magic! And no unfortunate clashing.

I've gotten over my anti-matching stance where shoes and outerwear are concerned, having discovered that it takes a lot more effort to find two different, exactly right, reasonably priced pairs of shoes or jackets than it does to find two different, decent-looking shirts.

That September, at a Mothers of Twins Club tag sale, I spent a stubborn fifteen minutes going from booth to booth, trying to find a second fall jacket for the girls. The first one I'd found—and fallen in love with—had a matching mate, but I turned my nose up at it. After zooming around in vain for a while, I finally told myself I was being ridiculous and went back to get other one.

"I wondered when you'd be back," the woman manning the booth said to me with a smile, handing the jacket to me.

They were the cutest and yet most practical jackets ever—the girls wore them for three whole seasons—and as long as they were wearing different pants, they didn't *really* look like they were dressed alike.

So these days, you can be sure that if the daughter of the woman across the street (and there is such a person), who dresses her twins alike, wants to give us two beautiful, matching, barely worn London Fog winter coats, approximate retail value $69.99, then I'll be damned if I'm going to go out and buy another, different-looking coat on principle.

And when friends or family members see the girls in matching coats or shoes and exclaim, in mock horror, "What is this? Matching clothes?!" I usually say something along the lines of "Yeah, yeah. Shut up."

I really do get the convenience of dressing twins alike, and God knows as parents of twins, we'll take as many shortcuts as we can get away with. I've also heard some parents say that dressing their twins alike makes it easier to keep track of them at crowded playgrounds, zoos, monster truck rallies, etc. I can see that, I guess. Nevertheless, I'll pass. Unless it's jacket weather.

And yet, as different as Elsa and Clio had always been and continued to be in temperament, in some things they were blessedly similar. This has been, for us, one of the great ironies of parenting twins: we really, really, really want the girls to feel like and grow as individuals. But we really, really, *really* want them to be OK with eating, sleeping, bathing, and engaging in various other everyday activities at exactly the same time, in pretty much exactly the same way. Because it's a helluva lot more convenient for us.

Take clothing size: while Elsa has always been taller and heavier than Clio, starting from just a few weeks after they were born, the two of them could always wear the same size diapers— this despite Elsa's more generous booty—and clothing. This meant we only had to keep one size of diaper on hand at any given time and could keep all of the girls' (mostly nonmatching, to be sure!) clothes in one big dresser to use interchangeably. (Although there were certain pieces that just seemed more inherently

"Clio" or "Elsa," which we would dress them in accordingly, and gradually they began to show preference for certain clothes themselves, which they'd start to think of as "mine" instead of "ours.")

We were also lucky when it came to getting the girls onto the same sleep schedule. The grand majority of the time they slept and napped in synch, or close to it. Clio had always needed a little less sleep—as was evident even in the womb, where she did far more constant Tae Kwon Do than her sister down on the bottom bunk—but it wasn't a major inconvenience.

At around twenty months old, though, Clio started exhibiting disturbing symptoms of morning person-ness. She started waking up a full hour (or more) before Elsa, and instead of playing or looking at books in her crib, as she sometimes had in the past, she initiated a new ritual: throwing her blanket, musical Gloworm doll (thunk!), books (thunk, thunk!), and pacifiers out of the crib with gusto, then proceeding to wail until we came in and got her. And because Elsa was almost always still sleeping—or looking groggily up at us as if to say, "would you get her the hell out of here?"—we'd take Clio into our bedroom and attempt to get her to lie in bed with us while we stole a few extra minutes of sleep.

But she was rarely interested. She'd sit up and start identifying parts of our faces, complete with full index finger to nostril penetration when she got to "nose." Then she'd climb down off the bed and start walking around the bedroom picking up random objects. Or—and this was the worst—she'd pitch a violent screaming fit for no apparent reason, absolutely inconsolable, and wake Elsa up in the process. And then we'd all be miserable and cranky.

Eventually we got into the habit of one of us going downstairs early with Clio while the other, and Elsa, slept. Usually Elsa was up by seven thirty or so, but one late summer morning she actually slept until eight forty-five: a new household record.

"Not fair," Alastair said as I waltzed happily into the kitchen, Elsa in my arms, and got myself a cup of coffee. It had been his turn to get up with Clio, and she had woken up even earlier than usual. "Not fair at all."

"Hey, you got to sleep in yesterday," I said.

"Not until almost *nine*."

"OK, I got lucky. But she slept until after eight yesterday."

"I know." He shook his head. "Man, if we just had Elsa, we'd be golden. Think of all the sleep we'd get."

"But," I offered, "we probably wouldn't appreciate it as much, because we wouldn't have the contrast of another baby getting up earlier."

"Yeah, no," he said. "I think I'd still appreciate it."

The girls began to diverge more sharply in other matters as well: Clio showed a growing preference for dolls and stuffed animals, while Elsa liked building and stacking toys. Clio became increasingly picky about what foods she would and wouldn't eat, while Elsa remained more or less omnivorous.

Actually, Clio became pickier in a lot of things. But let's not call it picky; let's call it discerning. Refined. Judicious. Let's assume that her insistence on having the darker of whichever two sippy cups we put on the table was a sign that one day she might be a celebrated painter, with an astounding eye for color. And let's decide that times when I gave her and Elsa completely identical objects to play with—whether that meant a rubber ball or a toilet paper tube—and she always wanted the one that I'd given Elsa, not the one I'd given her, it was because she is so supremely perceptive she notices things invisible to the average human eye. And when she threw loud, screaming fits when either Elsa or we didn't immediately cede to her demands, we told ourselves, "My, how passionate she is! What spirit! She'll make an excellent evangelical Baptist preacher someday!"

Likewise, when Elsa gleefully tackled her sister for "fun," causing her to cry, or climbed repeatedly up onto the dining table after we had told her (repeatedly) not to, we told ourselves, "She can't help it! She's a natural athlete! And just think of the college scholarships!"

We tried to tell ourselves, and each other, all sorts of things about our children's behavior in an attempt to stay positive and sane.

Other times—more of the time—we just told it like it was: we loved the girls to death, but they sure could be assho—that is, a challenge, sometimes.

16

When the depression hit for a third time that year, sideswiping me from completely out of nowhere when the girls were just shy of twenty-one months old, my reaction was something along the lines of, "You've got to be fucking kidding me."

One of Alastair's and my favorite movies has always been *Groundhog Day* with Bill Murray. A cranky, misanthropic weatherman, played by Murray, goes to a small town to cover the annual Groundhog Day celebration and finds himself, inexplicably, stuck in time: when he wakes up the next morning, it's Groundhog Day again—and he's the only one experiencing it as a repeat event. Next day, same thing. Over and over again, until he is so despondent that he tries to kill himself. But he can't. He keeps waking up the next—the same, that is—morning. Finally, he starts using his time in infinity more wisely, and eventually he is released.

"This movie," Alastair said once, shortly after recovering from his struggle with depression, back when we were in our early twenties, "is about what it's like to hit rock bottom."

I had never thought of it that way before; I'd just thought of the movie as something more along the lines of *A Christmas Carol*—supernatural forces help a person on the wrong track see the error of his ways and reform. But even though this episode of depression wouldn't actually turn out to be my rock bottom— that wouldn't happen for another year—now I understood what Alastair was talking about.

Every morning I woke up, hoping that this was the day I would feel better (*It was just a blip, a fluke! How could I be depressed again?*), to discover that, no, I was still here, down in the dirt, with the damned groundhogs.

And this time there hadn't been anything remotely resembling a triggering event. No big changes. No bad news. Although the economy was starting to fall apart, and our retirement accounts nosediving, my job, at least, appeared to be secure. The only direct impact the financial meltdown had on my life were layoffs within the publishing industry; my agent wanted to hold off on submitting my book anywhere new until the dust settled a bit. Which was frustrating, but not tragic.

Of course, the task of parenting two toddlers wasn't what you'd call a walk in the park. But for this challenge to plunge me, out of the blue, into depression didn't make a whole lot of sense.

I called my psychiatrist for an appointment, only to discover that—oops—the mental health network for my health insurance plan had changed and my doctor wasn't in the new one. I had to start from scratch. In between fuming about the health care system, finding a new shrink, and trying to get through my days, I googled things along the lines of "Can Prozac stop working?" Yes and no, said Doctor Google, as he almost always does when posed medical questions.

My real doctor—the new one I found—said the same thing.

He was a different bird than my previous shrink, much more focused on pharmacology than root, emotional causes. Which was A-OK with me. Anyway, root causes my ass. This episode of depression was out of the blue. No rhyme or reason to it. My drugs were not working, and I wanted a new one, or something. Shock therapy. Leeches. Bring it on.

"In most cases," this new doctor—gray mustachioed, serious, and bearing a fair resemblance to my sixth-grade math teacher—said, "'Prozac poopout,' in my opinion, isn't an indication that the fluoxetine has stopped working" (he prefers to call drugs by their pharmacological, not brand, names, because he hates the trend toward mass marketing of psychiatric drugs) "but an indication that you weren't on a high enough dose to begin with." He went on to say that in his experience, and in much of the new research coming out, the recommended doses of fluoxetine were lower than what many people with major depression needed.

"Fine," I said. "Dose me up."

And he did. And I waited for the relief to come.

I don't remember how long after that first increase it was that I called him back. Two weeks? Three?

All I remember is sitting on a bench near the parking garage at work, about to leave to go home because I couldn't make it through the day, crying, leaving a message on his voice mail saying, "I just can't keep suffering like this. I need something. I need some relief. Is there anything else we can do?"

His response was what I expected: give it a few more days. It takes a while for the effects to kick in. But just in case, he said, he'd write me a prescription for a drug called aripiprazole that I could try adding on, which for some people helped boost the effectiveness of drugs like fluoxetine.

"I hesitate even to mention the brand name," he said, "because it's one of the worst—bordering on smarmy, really. But they call it Abilify."

Totally smarmy.

And completely unhelpful in my case. The morning after I'd taken my second or third dose—a rainy, chilly October day—we decided to take the girls to the Museum of Science, along with all of the other parents of young children in the Greater Boston area, and parts of New Hampshire, Rhode Island, and Connecticut. There is an area there just for younger kids, full of things to touch and roll and observe and insert, all of them ostensibly to develop various pre-science and math skills and illustrate various scientific principles. Of course, this is entirely lost on anyone under three and more or less ignored by the parents, who are too busy chasing their children around to stop and ponder the laws of physics. Or, in my case, too completely zonked on aripiprazole to do much of anything besides wander around in a daze.

At one point, Alastair found me sitting on the floor looking mildly stoned while Clio played with a giant, illuminated peg board—like a supersized Lite-Brite. He asked me how I was feeling.

"I don't feel anything," I said. "It's like I have no inner monologue." I didn't realize this until I actually said it, not having any inner monologue. And the realization was rather disturbing. "I am never taking this drug again."

"Do you think maybe it takes a while to get used to it?"

I told him I didn't care; I'd rather just be depressed than depressed *and* lobotomized.

"Should we go home?" he asked.

"Yes, please," I said.

I did not take any more of the zombie pills, and at my next visit to my doctor, he upped my Prozac dose again. And I held onto hope that it was only a matter of time before I felt better, as I had every time before.

We spent that Halloween with Alastair's parents in the leafy, lovely New York suburb where they live. The girls' costumes were a reflection of the amount of energy and effort I had at that point: minimalist ballerinas. We already had pink tights, long-sleeved pink shirts, and little tutus that someone had given us as a baby shower gift way back when. I bought a couple of feathery pink clips for the girls' hair and called it a day. And no, I was not thrilled with myself for giving them both the same costume, but they didn't care, and I was going for expediency. As it turned out, though, Clio solved the issue by refusing to wear the tutu or hair clip. So we had one very pretty ballerina and one very chic modern dancer. Perfect.

And it was actually quite a lovely evening—cool but not cold. Lots of kids out and about. The girls actually sort of got the whole trick-or-treating concept, to our surprise: they said "tweeee!" (as in, "treeeeat!") each time we approached a door, and when we got home, they pulled the classic, time-honored kid move of dumping all their candy out onto the floor and trying to steal from each other's piles.

As we drove back up to Boston the next morning, I continued to feel relatively good—not great, mind you, but good—and thought: hey, maybe I'm starting to turn a corner here.

But then I got a little too cocky. That afternoon, back at home, I volunteered to take the girls with me to the grocery store.

Which may go down in history, along with the perm I got in seventh grade, as one of the worst decisions I've ever made.

Even Alastair thought maybe it was too much for me to handle, given how I'd been feeling. But we needed milk and bread and bananas, and it was something to pass the time until dinner, and I thought I should ride the positive momentum: push myself, in hopes that it would jolt the depression out of my system.

I somehow seemed to have forgotten that going to the grocery store with two toddlers is something that should be done only in the direst of emergencies.

We'd barely made it halfway through the produce section when Clio started whining and crying to get out of the cart, then yelling for milk or water or juice (which I stupidly hadn't brought). Then she started screaming for a cookie. Elsa, meanwhile, kept wriggling out of the seat belt—it was one of those shopping carts shaped like a little car—and standing up with half her body out the front window like a Labrador retriever with a death wish.

Had I felt normal, I could have coped. I would have felt stressed out and annoyed, no doubt. But it wouldn't have felt like a tragedy. I wouldn't have felt a wall of dread spring up in front of my face every time I had to speak or push the cart forward or find the next item on my list.

As we made our loud and riotous way through the store, I could sense people looking at us, maybe in pity, maybe annoyance, maybe some in smiling, "how cute they are, but what a handful" sympathy. But I kept my gaze straight ahead and told myself not to get overwhelmed: just take it step by step. Get everything on the list; get out and go home. And then what? Unload the groceries, keep the girls entertained for another hour and a half, make them dinner, get them to bed, make our dinner, unpack, go to bed, drag myself to work in the morning. When would there be relief?

I half-wished I would collapse right there in the cereal aisle and wake up in a sanatorium—maybe out in the Berkshires somewhere, the kind where they used to send ladies suffering from "nervous exhaustion." Birds singing. Clean white sheets. A rocking chair. Nothing to do but sit and stare out the window.

But I didn't collapse. Because this is the blessing and the curse of serious but not devastating depression: you feel completely awful, but not *so* completely awful that you can't function.

So I did what I had to do. Specifically, I tore open a package of Fig Newtons and handed them to Elsa and Clio at regular intervals until I got up to the checkout.

At the bank branch up at the front of the store, there was a long line of people—immigrants, day laborers, people who clearly struggled to make ends meet—waiting to cash checks. Young men, mothers with kids, old people. From the corner of my eye I could see them smiling with kindness and amusement at the spectacle of us—this harried young woman and this adorable, miserable pair of toddlers. And though it's not who I am, and not what I would normally do, I rolled right past them toward the exits, grim-faced, fast, angry, not acknowledging a single smile. Hating myself for feeling so miserable when I had every reason to be happy, while those people had it so much worse.

The girls whined and cried all the way home, and when I got inside I wailed to Alastair to please come down and get the groceries out of the car and put them away. He looked at me and said, "What happened?"

I broke down sobbing. "It was awful," I said. As if I'd just survived a war, not a trip to Stop & Shop.

The girls stood watching, uncharacteristically silent. Clio looked particularly confused and concerned.

"Mommy's sad," Alastair explained. They knew "sad." Sort of.

I sat down in our big, creaky recliner and Elsa crawled up into my lap. She grinned and giggled and smacked her little hand just a little too hard, as was her way, against my wet cheek. "Mommy sad," she said.

At this, I cried even harder.

It was one thing to be depressed with babies—needy, but more or less oblivious to the moods of people around them. Now I had toddlers, who were every day more cognizant of and engaged in the world around them. I didn't want them to see me like this. I didn't want them to be frightened. I was frightened by my father's tears when he was in the depths of his own depression, and I was sixteen. How unsettling must it be to a small child to see her mother weep?

So I pulled myself together. "Yeah," I said, and managed a smile. "Mommy's sad. But you make me feel better."

Just not at the grocery store.

On November 5, 2008, while the girls napped, I watched election coverage videos online: highlights from Obama's victory speech and McCain's gracious concession. College students on campuses around the country rushing out into the streets. People in cities—black people, white people, young people, old people—dancing and shouting.

I'd woken up too early, like a kid on Christmas morning, and couldn't fall back asleep. I probably should have snuck in a nap while the girls were sleeping, but I couldn't. I wanted to keep reveling in the excitement and possibility of what had happened.

The girls woke up while I was mid-video, and I ignored them a little longer than I probably should have. In an interesting reversal of roles, Elsa was the one champing at the bit to get out of her crib and enjoy the rest of the afternoon, while Clio was acting sleepy and sulky. I let Clio hang out in her crib a few minutes longer and brought Elsa into my office, where we watched the rest of the video I'd been looking at: the crowd in Grant Park, erupting upon hearing the news that Obama was the projected winner.

Elsa clapped her hands and grinned and yelled, "Yay! Yay!"

And I said, "Yes, yay! Something really exciting happened!" Someday, I thought, maybe she would understand just how exciting it was. But then it occurred to me that Elsa and Clio, and millions of other children like them, might never really comprehend the jubilation that much of our country, and the world, experienced that night.

They won't have lived through the fear and division of the previous eight years. The first American president they'll know and remember, for the rest of their lives, will be an African American man. They'll think it's the norm. They'll think, "Why was it such a big deal?" And that, in some ways, is a beautiful thing.

I'd been getting teary and emotional all day, and watching the videos was no exception. I cried as I held Elsa on my lap. Smiled and laughed and cried and rocked. I still felt the depression; it was there, the tightness in my chest. But I was able to co-opt it that day as a feeling of positive emotion. I could assign it fullness and joy.

When Elsa looked up and saw my tears, she put her little palm (splat!) against my face and said, "Mommy sad?"

"No," I told her, and smiled like I hadn't in weeks. "Mommy's very, very happy."

17

Soon enough, I was happy for real. And just in time for the holidays. God bless fluoxetine! God bless my new shrink! God bless us, everyone!

Ever since I was in my late teens, when the luster of the holidays began to dull and I started harboring powerful nostalgia about the Christmases of my childhood, I looked forward to sharing Christmas with my future children—to give them that magical experience and relive it vicariously. This started well before I was in the mind-set of having children. It even persisted through a period of a couple of years when I wasn't sure I *wanted* children. I would have had kids just to give them Christmas. I loved the holiday that much.

Same with Thanksgiving, and even Hanukkah, which I never celebrated with my family, being brought up Christian, but which I had fond memories of sampling when the moms of the Jewish kids at my elementary school brought in latkes, applesauce, and dreidels. And there was always the obligatory Hanukkah song for school holiday concerts—something jaunty in a minor key.

Alastair's mother is Jewish, so we celebrated Hanukkah with his parents and the girls that year. It's safe to say that the whole thing went well over their small heads. They thought the menorah was a birthday cake.

Likewise, they were basically oblivious to the notion (and certainly the meaning) of Christmas, although they did enjoy "helping" decorate the tree. They also loved—I mean, really, really loved—the animatronic singing snowmen, Santas, and other creatures that my parents keep sadistically buying for us. And they certainly enjoyed getting presents.

The biggest hit of all was the two pink doll strollers, which quickly became the vehicles of choice for transporting the Curious George dolls that the girls' babysitter had given them. Two toddlers whizzing around the house with monkeys in strollers on Christmas morning is a heartwarming sight. Until, just as you sit down with a nice cup of coffee and a slice of coffee cake, thinking how great it is that they're playing on their own and congratulating yourself for getting them such an awesome gift, they both try to get through the doorway to the kitchen at the same time, the wheels of the strollers get tangled up, and they start whining and crying and yelling. And you realize, with a sense of cold, creeping dread, that this is going to happen pretty much every time they play with the damned things, and maybe you should have just gotten them an easel: two sides, no contact, no fighting.

What's more, it isn't long before they start brawling over whose stroller is whose, and whose monkey is whose, and you find yourself resorting to those god-awful, obnoxious animatronic dolls to distract them: *Hey guys, look! The snowmen want to sing to you!* It doesn't work, so now the snowmen are singing, in their terrible, nasal, electronic voices *and* the girls are still yelling. After this cacophonous crisis is resolved, you sink back into your chair and ask your husband if 10:00 A.M. is too early to start drinking.

"We should probably wait until ten thirty," he says.

A few weeks earlier Alastair and I had actually snagged a bit of extended respite from the increasing intensity of twin toddler parenting. The day after Thanksgiving we left the girls at my parents' house in southern Maine—Alastair's parents were staying there, too—and escaped for a night at a bed and breakfast up the coast in Camden. It was the first time we'd been away from the girls together for more than a few hours.

And what a strange and lovely sensation it was to find ourselves temporarily transported back to our life before children. Except it wasn't that life, entirely, because we still talked and thought about the girls. I still had deflated breasts and a flabby tummy. And we were relishing the time a lot more than we would have, I think, if it were five years earlier, when we did this sort of thing fairly frequently.

Still, we lapsed into—rather, sank happily back into like a feather mattress—the things we used to do and the way we used to interact as a younger couple. We browsed in shops, ate more frequently than was biologically necessary, talked about everything from our college days to our future plans to how Abraham Lincoln won the Republican nomination. (Alastair was reading a Lincoln biography at the time. Not that that makes our conversation any less dorky.) We were silly and stupid and flirty and tender.

As we were falling asleep in our quiet room at the B&B, in our big bed—and I mean really big, with a step stool and everything—Alastair said, "Who's getting up with the girls in the morning?"

After an instant of dread—shit, we were having so much fun, it would really be nice to sleep in, and wasn't it his turn anyway?—came the relief of realization: no kids here. We could both sleep in. Hallefuckinglujah.

"You had to think about that for a minute didn't you?" Alastair said.

"Yeah." I laughed. "It's so weird. And so nice."

"Let's sleep forever," he suggested.

"Or at least until the last possible minute before they stop serving breakfast."

We got back to my parents' house at around five the next day. We'd been gone for just over twenty-four hours, but it felt like days. We were eager to see the girls, though we probably could have suffered through another night away.

But what a welcome we got when we came home. The girls greeted us with bright smiles and exclamations ("Mommy Daddy here!"), let us kiss them, and then—within approximately ten minutes of our arrival—had total screaming meltdowns. Both of them.

"They were perfectly happy the whole time you were gone!" one or more of the assembled grandparents exclaimed.

This is a phrase that I've come to loathe, particularly when uttered by the grandparents. Perhaps they mean it in their own defense, as in: *We weren't torturing and neglecting your children while you were gone, we promise! This isn't our fault!* But this thought leads directly into the meaning that I *do* take from it: that somehow it's *our* fault. That we must be doing something wrong as parents, otherwise our children wouldn't behave this way. Ever.

"This happens sometimes when they haven't seen us in a while," I said, trying in vain to hold and comfort a writhing Elsa (who I think was pissed because we'd put the kibosh on a second cookie after dinner). It was true; there had been plenty of times when I'd come home after a long day at work and the girls would suddenly completely break down, especially if they were in a fragile state—teething or getting over a cold.

And I fully believe that most children behave better with adults that they don't see and interact with on a frequent basis, i.e., grandparents. I also believe that kids are generally needier and more demanding around their own parents—particularly parents of the maternal persuasion.

I believed these things, but that belief wasn't strong enough to outweigh the fact that, on some level, I really did think it was my fault that my children were writhing around on the ground at my feet, inconsolable.

Everything about parenting was becoming much more difficult, it seemed. There was more whining, more crying, more defiance, and more fighting. There was more noise. Much, much more noise. And my confidence in my twin parenting skills, specifically those that had to do with double-duty chaos containing, limit setting, and tantrum taming, was seriously on the wane.

I hesitate to use the term "terrible twos" because there was so much that was absolutely precious about the girls at this time.

It's a remarkable age, really: the language development, the growing curiosity and interaction with the world, the beginnings of pretend play, and the downright cuteness. We have wonderful pictures and videos of Elsa and Clio at this age, dressing themselves up in our hats and scarves, twirling around to music in the living room and sitting peacefully at their miniature table in the middle of the kitchen, feet dangling under their chairs, playing with Play-Doh or finger painting. They were cuddly and giggly and affectionate, and delighted in tickling and flarfels (our term for a raspberry on the tummy) and being bounced on our knees for "trot, trot to Boston" and other horse-related rhymes.

They were also getting to the point where, if we got them started on an activity, they'd keep at it on their own for some time, with minimal need for parental intervention. It wasn't easy to come up with ideas, especially in the dead of winter. But every once in a while I'd devise some low-cost, superfun activity and would briefly feel like the world's greatest mother, ever.

There was, for example, the bean box: an ordinary wooden box that I filled with assorted dried beans. I would put the box down on the kitchen floor, along with plastic shovels, spoons, coffee cans, bowls, and other implements, and the girls would lose themselves in bean scooping and pouring. Or, they'd just sit in the box and give each other bean "baths." Cleanup was easy: I just swept up the loose beans and dumped them back into the box (along with whatever else was on the kitchen floor, but no matter). Bonus: if we are ever starving to death, I'm quite confident that we could move the refrigerator and stove and find at least eight ounces of stray black, pinto, white, and kidney beans underneath.

While the girls were engrossed in something like the bean box, all was right with the world. I could help them as needed, marvel at their dexterity and imagination (a bean bath! brilliant!), and even sneak in an e-mail or a little Facebook fun.

But the rest of the time was harder.

In the months just before and after their second birthday, the girls got it into their small heads that they were, basically, high queens and sovereigns of our house and that Alastair and I were their valet and maidservant, respectively. We tried very hard to disabuse them of this notion, but were not terribly successful.

Our co-queens had many demands: They wanted to play with Play-Doh *now*. They wanted more milk *now*. They wanted to watch the *Baby Animal Songs* DVD for the fourth time that day. They wanted me to read *Chicka Boom* for the fifth.

Queen Clio's most frequent demand was that we hold her. We tried to oblige when we could, but it wasn't always possible for obvious reasons: making breakfast, going to the bathroom, playing with your other child, etc. are all fairly tricky when you've got a twenty-six-pound person in your arms.

Clio was also very specific about how and where she wanted to be held: standing up vs. sitting down, with Mommy vs. with Daddy, in the kitchen or in the living room. She most definitely didn't like to share a lap with Elsa.

And when we said no, she didn't just cry a little and then lose steam. She would cry and yell and scream as if someone was sticking pins into her. *Through* her. When it got really out of hand, we'd put her upstairs in her crib for a while to chill out, but no sooner did we bring her back downstairs than the demands began anew.

We would explain that Mommy (or Daddy, as the case may have been) was doing something else and couldn't pick her up right then. We'd tell her she was a big girl who needed to walk / play / etc. by herself sometimes. We promised to pick her up later. We tried to distract her with toys or books or milk or nonlethal kitchen utensils. We tried pretty much everything. We were successful maybe 25 percent of the time.

Elsa had her share of fits, too, but she specialized in whining— a more low-grade but equally grating toddler behavior. She whined when she wanted a snack, she whined when we said no to something (e.g., the snack she'd just whined for), she whined when we interrupted her play because it was time to put shoes and coats on and go somewhere. And, worst of all, she whined when she wanted attention while we were occupied with the demands and tantrums of Queen Clio.

Which brings us to the heart of why so much of the time we felt so overwhelmed and exhausted and stressed out: twins.

Freakin' twins.

Let no one tell you parenting young twins is twice as hard as parenting one kid at a time. It is easily 2.5 times as hard. Maybe 2.8.

You've got two children at the exact same developmental stage, with more or less the same needs and demands, both wanting and needing various forms of attention at the same time. Even when both Alastair and I were there, it was exhausting.

During this period of the girls' lives, I frequently felt like I was groping my way through the dark when it came to managing their more challenging and exasperating behaviors. I was fumbling and bumbling with no clear sense of what the "right" way was to proceed. How much of the girls' behavior could we manage or improve, and how much of it was just inevitable two-ness? (And by that I mean both their age and their number.) Should we be giving them "time outs" for misbehavior, or were they too young for it to really work? Were our kids this intense because of something we were doing wrong, or was it just their personalities?

One thing I did know was that we were supposed to choose our battles. Problem is, it wasn't always clear which battles to choose. When was it right to stand firm and say no, and when did it make more sense to appease and thereby avoid a meltdown? Because once our girls—and Clio in particular—crossed the toddler Rubicon into the land of the screaming tantrum, there was no hope of getting them to calm down. Giving them back the crayons we took away, picking them back up after we put them down against their wishes, letting them eat that damned second cookie that we should have just let them have in the first place—useless. They were lost to us, lost to the world. And if they both went into tantrum mode at the same time—well, let's not even go there.

In retrospect, I think we probably did give in too easily, too often. And I think we should have been more consistent about what kinds of battles we would and wouldn't fight. Wanting to hear "Nanaphone" three times in a row? Sure, whatever, not worth fighting. Refusing to eat anything on their dinner plates and demanding applesauce instead? Stand firm, Mama. They're hardly going to starve to death.

But I also think that our girls were and are particularly spirited kids. And I also think we should have gone a bit easier on ourselves. We were doing the best we could.

Sometimes we had enough perspective to remind ourselves of this. Like the January night not long after the girls' second birthday, when Alastair and I were headed out to a gig he was playing at a local bar.

We'd beaten a hasty retreat from home as soon as the babysitter showed up. It had been a long, tiring day. We had gone to brunch at some friends' house that morning but had gotten a late start, and the usual mad rush to get the girls ready and out the door was even madder. Alastair couldn't find his glasses; I couldn't find my cell phone. We were tense and snippy with each other, bickering over one thing and another—who was supposed to pack up the diaper bag, who should have gotten the girls ready sooner, who was supposed to have looked up the directions to our friends' house, and who was undermining the other's parenting. The girls, little seismographs that they are, picked up on our tension and ratcheted up their own kvetching.

Once brunch was under way and our girls were playing contentedly with our friends' kids, things were fine. But when we got home, Clio didn't nap; the afternoon was long and dull; and Alastair and I still hadn't fully forgiven each other for what we each viewed as the other's unreasonableness in the morning.

The only brief bright spot of the day was when Alastair stayed home with Elsa and practiced his set and I took Clio to the grocery store. It was so easy, so simple, so delightful and calm and fun that I found myself almost in tears at times. Clio pointed out things on the shelves and stared, starry-eyed, at the bright lights overhead. I made the cart go fast and she giggled with squeaky glee. I felt acutely fond of her, in a way I hadn't in a long time.

So much of being with the girls lately, I realized, came down to crowd control. As a result, I rarely had the chance to *enjoy* each of the girls as individuals. Here in the frozen food aisle, I could. Which was wonderful—but shot through with sadness. Because I knew that when I got home, it would be back to the twin dynamic: both of the girls vying for my attention, and me unable to fully please—or truly appreciate—either of them.

I drove home feeling painfully jealous of my friends with just one kid, or even two kids of different ages.

That night, in the cold car, on the way to our night of music and beer and greasy burgers and conversation with friends— all of which we were looking forward to with desperate, happy anticipation—Alastair and I apologized to each other for the morning's nastiness. We didn't immediately feel warm and fuzzy toward each other, but the words had been spoken, at least, which was the first step.

We were both quiet for a moment, and then Alastair said, "You know, when our friends say to us, 'having twins must be so hard, and I don't know how you do it,' we're always so careful to say, 'well, having two or more kids at different ages is just as hard.' But you know what? Fuck that. Having two two-year-olds is ridiculous."

I loved him so much at that moment.

He was absolutely right: we commiserated with each other aplenty, but we rarely stepped back together to say, look: this is really, *really* hard. And we're doing the best we can.

The rest of the evening felt like more of break, emotionally, than I'd had in a long time. I gave myself permission to go easy on myself and enjoy this escape fully. And all the pieces fell into place for a perfect night out: We got a parking place right in front of the bar. Alastair played well and a good crowd showed up, including some friends we hadn't seen in a while. I enjoyed an exquisitely greasy burger and ate too many curly fries.

When we got home, the sitter reported that everything went fine, except that Elsa had a fit about sitting in her high chair. Not surprising, but nice that for once it wasn't my problem.

Before I got ready for bed myself, I went into the girls' room as I did (and still do) every night, to touch their cheeks and pull their blankets up over them.

And the next morning at seven sharp, when I heard Clio calling "Mommmmmy!" from her crib, tired as I was, I didn't groan and bury my head in my pillow. I smiled to myself and got up right away.

Because I just couldn't wait to see the little buggers.

18

Picture it: a cold, gray February day in the Greater Boston area.

A family in a Subaru Forester: a handsome father with a mischievous smile; a gorgeous—like, movie star, drop-dead gorgeous—mother who looks extremely good for her age; and two adorable two-year-old twin girls, all fresh from Tiny Tots swimming lessons at the local Boys and Girls Club, on their way home. It's midmorning, and tummies are grumbling.

One of the adorable twins—whose name is (adorably) Clio—says, in her loud but adorable little voice, "I wanna eat fishies!"

The gorgeous mother knows, of course, that she means Pepperidge Farm goldfish crackers, not *actual* fish, because fish is not on the list of seven beige foods that her children prefer at this juncture: bread, cheese, yogurt, applesauce, bananas, crackers, and pasta.

"OK, Clio," says the gorgeous mother. "When we get home, we'll have some fishy crackers."

At this point the other adorable twin, Elsa, chimes in: "I wanna eat fishies, too!"

"OK," the gorgeous mother repeats in her calm, nurturing, and oh-so-patient way. "Fishy crackers for everyone!"

And then the children, because they have no understanding of the laws of physics, and therefore do not understand that it takes *time* to drive from one place (swim class) to another (home) proceed to repeat their requests for fishy crackers.

The handsome father, at this point, tells the girls that, yep, they're going to get fishy crackers when they get home, but they need to be patient (a concept that the twins—while extremely bright—have yet to grasp), and please stop asking.

But the girls aren't listening.

"No, Elsa," Clio is saying. "CLIO eat fishies!"

"Elsa eat fishies, too!"

"No, Elsa. Dat not nice! Clio eat da fishies!"

Elsa starts to cry, with great, tragic passion. "Nooo!! Elsa want fishies!!"

Now Clio is crying, too. "No! Clio eat fishies! Clio eat fishies!"

At which point the mother twists around in her seat—a maneuver she is so accustomed to doing in the car by this point that the muscles on the left side of her back are more pliable than those on the right, leading to a slight postural distortion that, fortunately, does not significantly detract from her beauty and grace—and tries to explain to the girls that they can *both* have fishy crackers. Just because one of them has fishy crackers it doesn't mean that the other once can't. There are plenty of fishy crackers to go around.

This doesn't accomplish a damned thing.

At which point the mother calmly asks the handsome father

to please pull the car over. She'd like to walk the rest of the way home.

To be fair, if I try to put myself in the very small shoes of a two-year-old twin, I can almost sort of understand what was behind an absurdist argument like this one. And what lay at the root of the fits frequently being pitched around this time over whose sippy cup or bowl was whose, or who got to go up the stairs first.

The drama of toddlerhood is all about the constant tension between wanting more control and not having the verbal ability to ask for it, or the emotional maturity to accept the fact that you can't always have it. I imagine that when you have a twin, this person who's always there, and who needs and wants the exact same thing, it's that much harder. Every day, every waking minute, that other little person is there, competing for the things *you* want.

So is it any wonder that you feel a little threatened by the thought of someone else moving in on your fishy crackers?

Parenting twins is not for the faint of heart, but neither, I suspect, is being one. Of course, at two years old, the girls didn't quite "get" yet that they were twins.

Our philosophy all along was not to fetishize or make a big deal out of the girls' twin-ness. But now that they were more verbal, we started occasionally talking about the fact that they were twins, usually in reference to the other sets of twins we knew and had occasional playdates with: *Ethan and Emmett are twins just like you! Milo and Amelia are twins, just like you!* Etc.

But most of their friends at that time (that is to say the children of our friends that we forced them to play with) were singletons, without siblings. And I did wonder if, when Elsa and Clio played with them, they wondered where the "other one" was. As far as they were concerned, being a twin was just the normal way to be.

It wasn't actually until Elsa and Clio were well into their threes that they began to have a sense of what it meant to be a twin: they were both in Mommy's tummy at the same time, they were born on the same day, and therefore they had the same birthday. As of this writing, they're still content to leave it at that.

But as they get older, surely there will be more questions: Does that mean we're exactly the same? Who's older? How come not everybody has a twin?

And then there might come the stickier questions: Do you love one of us more? And *why* are we twins?

Not that this last one will be an issue for quite some time, given that it requires a fundamental understanding of the facts of life. But I suspect that at some point, if they ask, we'll tell our girls that we had help getting pregnant. It's not on par with telling children that they're adopted, but I do wonder if it's a difficult subject to broach, and one fraught with all kinds of existential questions: Was I "unnatural"? Do you wish you hadn't had twins? Was one of us a mistake? What if we weren't really supposed to be born?

The older Elsa and Clio get, and the more "big" questions they ask—as I write this, the girls are four, and very curious about death—the more I am aware of how difficult it can be to give your children the answers they're after, whether for lack of answers (how confusing it must be for them to be told that I don't know what happens to people after they die, when I know the answers to almost everything else they ask) or for lack of answers that a child could really understand. How could I ever explain, for example, that while I never really wanted twins, and was even disappointed when I first learned I was having them, I really *do* want them—Elsa and Clio, born together—and can't possibly imagine it any other way?

It was—have I mentioned?—a challenging time in the parenting scheme of things. But still, big picture, I felt remarkably content.

One afternoon in late February, I went over to my friend Polly's house for a cup of coffee—she has a son six months younger than the girls, but I had consciously decided *not* to bring the girls so we could actually have a conversation—and when she asked how I'd been, depression- and mood-wise, I told her I was doing well. Really, really well.

"That's great," she said. "So, is anything going on with your book?"

"Not really," I told her. "My agent still feels like it's not a great time to be sending it out. But she's trying to pull together a list of people for a next big push. I'm not getting my hopes up, though. It's all so beyond my control anyway."

"And are you writing anything else? Besides your blog? You were going to start another novel, right?"

I shrugged. "No, but I'm OK with taking a break for a while. With the girls being at such a tough age, and work and everything. I feel like maybe this just isn't my time to be trying to write. But I know I'll go back to it."

"Oh." She seemed vaguely puzzled by my equanimity. "And work? Are you still thinking of freelancing?"

In a conversation we had had several months earlier, I had

told her that I felt conflicted about my job. Although it was only twenty-five to thirty hours a week, I still felt like I might prefer the flexibility and independence of being a freelancer instead. It might afford me more time to write and to be with the girls.

"Eventually, yes," I told her. "But it would be crazy for me to jump ship in this economy. I don't know. I'm just really content with where I am right now. I feel almost Zen-like about my life."

"Wow. That's great," she said, although in retrospect, she sounded slightly skeptical.

But the way I saw it, I had friends and financial security and a beautiful family. I had my health—I wasn't depressed anymore, no sirree. I was exactly where I was supposed to be, doing exactly what I was supposed to be doing. To quote the "Desiderata" of Max Ehrmann, the universe was unfolding exactly as it should.

It was right around this time that I entered my novel in the Amazon Breakthrough Novel contest. When it advanced to the second round, I used social networking to rally friends and family (and their friends and family) to download the excerpt and write reviews. I didn't expect to win, but hoped that if I could generate enough buzz around the book and prove that I had a readership, it might be a good selling point for my agent in approaching a few more editors. Ultimately, I got over a hundred reviews, and so many downloads that my novel excerpt actually climbed as high as number 60 on the Amazon bestseller list. It was pretty exciting. And I felt pretty charged up. (On top of Zen-like.)

As my feelings of happiness, confidence, and energy continued to intensify, I did once mention to Alastair that maybe, just maybe, I was a *little* bit too happy, and I worried that it didn't bode well. After all, two of the last three times I'd been depressed, it had come in the midst of my feeling particularly happy and energized—my trip to the literary conference in New York the year before, and then the final edits and first submissions of my book.

One Thursday evening after a run, I said to Alastair, as I did my stretches on the living room rug, "You know, it's weird. I kind of feel like I'm on a little bit of a high." My endorphins usually kicked in when I ran, and, listening to my own personal sound track on my iPod as I went, it was hard not to feel supremely good. And I'd definitely felt that way and then some on this particular run. But I wasn't just referring to that. It had been a few weeks now of steadily rising mood.

"You don't feel manic, do you?" Alastair asked, with hesitation.

"No, I don't think so," I said. Mania was not being able to sleep, talking too fast and too loud, doing things excessively and impulsively, having delusions of omnipotence. But that wasn't me, or what was going on here.

Still, I did feel like maybe things were getting a bit too amped up, too intense.

Then, in mid-March, as if I was just begging the circumstances of my first depressive crash a year earlier to repeat themselves, I went to New York for a solo weekend. This time it was to visit my two best friends from high school, one of whom had recently had a baby. And it was on this trip when I realized, without a doubt, that I was way too happy.

Taking the train to the city for a weekend away from your kids to bum around with the two people you love the most in the world and who remind you of more carefree days is, indeed, a totally fun thing to do. But extraordinary? Miraculous? Magical?

Well, you say, sure, maybe. When you don't get out on your

own much—which I certainly didn't—stepping onto a train and chug-chug-chugging off to the big city to see your best pals is arguably a pretty exhilarating thing. OK, fair enough.

But when I got onto that train in the morning and sat there in my window seat drinking my coffee and eating the awesomest raisin bagel in the universe (I can still almost taste it) and we pulled away from the station, I looked up at the bright red of the brick buildings of the leather district against the cerulean sky, light glinting off their tall windows, and was nearly overcome by a sense of beauty, of promise, of assurance that God was in His heaven and all was right with the word.

I thought to myself: I have never been happier than this moment. I felt that perhaps, by being utterly accepting of where I was in my life, and living so presently in the moment, I'd achieved a sort of enlightenment. That perhaps I'd discovered—although I couldn't quite articulate it (which was sort of the point)—the meaning of life.

I spent most of the train ride down to the city alternately marveling at the great mystery and beauty of existence, rapidly scribbling down ideas for new writing projects and marketing tactics for my book, and reading a novel by Ian McEwan, *On Chesil Beach,* which I'm sure would have been great anyway—he's one of my favorite writers—but which, that day, seemed exquisite (though I had trouble staying focused on it for more than a few minutes at a time).

The train ride home was equally absurdly sublime. I spent much of it looking out the window as the train emerged from the engineering marvels that were the tracks beneath Manhattan into the rich patchwork of humanity, in all its beauty and squalor, that was Harlem and the Bronx; through the suburban haven of Westchester, whence my husband came; through my Connecticut hometown, past the condominium complex where my late grandmother had lived, past my middle school and then the church that four generations of my family had attended. I found myself crying—literally, seriously crying—at the beauty and tragedy and *lif*eness of it all. Crying and smiling and laughing. I felt overcome. Euphoric.

When I got home I told Alastair that I was definitely, *definitely* too happy. Something didn't feel quite right.

"I'm worried I'm going to crash," I told him.

Several days later, I did. Except it wasn't quite the sort of crash I'd expected: I didn't feel lethargic and tired and listless. I didn't even feel unhappy, exactly. Instead, I felt anxious, disoriented, disjointed, oversensitive, my moods bouncing here and there, pinball-like. On one occasion—when, unfortunately, I happened to be speaking on a panel to Harvard undergrads about the pros and cons of getting an MFA in creative writing—I had the strange sensation that my mind was coming apart at the seams. My thoughts and even my words seemed to be drifting outward in all directions, and I worried that at any minute I might slip into incoherence. "Holding it together" felt like precisely, literally what I was doing. It was an almost out-of-body experience.

I'd already made an appointment to see my doctor at that point, but the earliest opening he'd had wasn't for two more weeks. I called him that night after the panel, sitting in my car in the parking garage, because for some reason I felt the need to call immediately. I told him I had to see him sooner—something very strange was going on, and I needed his help.

He called me back the next morning and told me that he couldn't understand what I'd said on my message—I was talking too fast.

. . .

When I saw my doctor several days later—he found a way to
fit me in—he confirmed what I suspected and what some Internet sleuthing of my own had suggested: at some point I'd hopped
from the monopolar spectrum onto the bipolar one. I didn't have
the classic kind of bipolar disorder one hears the most about,
with major manic episodes. It was a milder form called bipolar II.

With bipolar II, there's no mania in the severe, potentially
life-threatening sense. Instead, there's hypomania—a low-level
form of mania frequently characterized by high energy and feelings of extreme confidence, creativity, and productivity.

In other words, pretty good stuff.

"If we could bottle it up and sell it," my psychiatrist joked,
"we'd make a fortune."

In many cases bipolar II depression is never diagnosed as such
because the hypomania is mild enough that people don't recog-
nize it. (Hell, how could happiness, creativity, and discovering
the meaning of life feel like a *bad* thing?) Sometimes it's barely
discernible at all.

To further confuse and obfuscate the matter—and this is the
Big Ironic Clincher—antidepressants like Prozac can actually
cause rapid cycling and mania. So while we were upping my
medication doses in an attempt to get out ahead of my depression, we were actually making things *worse*. Woo hoo!

So the first thing we had to do from a pharmaceutical standpoint was decrease my dose of antidepressants while adding in a
new kind of drug, a mood stabilizer. But the first thing I had
to do from a psychological standpoint was try to wrap my head
around this new diagnosis and what it meant.

I knew—I really did know—that bipolar II was a different animal from bipolar I and that my case was probably on the pretty mild end of the spectrum at that. But I was still a little freaked out.

The only person with bipolar that I'd ever known well was my aunt—my mother's sister—and she has a severe case. When she is in a manic state, she's hard to follow—her thoughts seem to chain one to the next, jutting sharply and unexpectedly in new directions, flying off onto tangents, and looping back around again with a logic that's difficult if not impossible to follow. Although I have no doubt that it all makes sense to her, much in the same way someone who's been smoking pot or doing mushrooms feels like every crazy thing they think and say—and everything their similarly stoned friends are saying—is profoundly and miraculously interconnected. (Not that I know this from personal experience or anything.)

But my aunt's benign mania frequently develops into something darker and more fearful. She feels overwhelmed with worry and anxiety and generally confused, prone to making illogical connections (e.g., because she didn't pay her credit card bill on time, the mailman will stop coming). She even has episodes of psychosis—delusions and severe paranoia. Once, she was convinced that her boyfriend at the time had taken her ATM card and was stealing money from her account. He hadn't, of course, but there was no telling her that.

The flip side of her mania is, of course, depression. And when she's in that state, she can barely function at all. It's been years since she's been able to work.

Is it any wonder I was afraid of having the word "bipolar"—no matter how lightly it applied—used to describe me? What if my problems worsened? The idea of not being able to work, not being able to be there for my children and husband, not being able to be the incredibly functional person I have always been was too terrible even to imagine.

My doctor said that provided we found the right treatment, my prognosis was good. There was nothing to suggest that my condition would deteriorate. And I knew, of course, that plenty of people lived their whole lives with bipolar disorders and did absolutely fine. But still. If my flavor and severity of depression had changed once, who was to say it wouldn't change again?

I was ashamed, too. Just having depression—as stigmatized as that is—seemed like the common cold compared to bipolar. People got depressed all the time, to varying degrees. But bipolar disorder—that was kissing cousins with *crazy*. It was the kind of mental illness (not just depression—a *mental illness!*) that could send people running down the street naked or jumping off buildings believing they can fly. Would I end up there someday? Naked or flying? Flying naked?

And yet, despite the strangeness and mild shock of having this new diagnosis on my medical charts, there was a part of me that was relieved. Now, at least, we had an explanation for why I'd kept going in and out of depression. We knew what we were dealing with. And we could tackle it the right way.

If I could handle two babies, I could handle two mood poles, right?

Right.

Eventually.

19

How steeped in dualities life felt at that time. Two mood states—and, now, two different drugs to regulate them; we scaled back the Prozac and added a mood stabilizer. Two toddlers, both two years old, to boot. Half the time, very, very good; half the time, horrid. One with her father's eyes, one with her mother's. One introvert, one extrovert.

But wait. Back up. Was it fair or even accurate for me to label Elsa a Myers-Briggs E and Clio an I, or were they only so in comparison to one another? Furthermore, did we only tend to think of them as such because, as human beings, we have such a strong inclination toward dividing things neatly into opposing pairs? Good or bad, male or female, manic or depressive.

Elsa was indeed outgoing and quick to warm up to new places and people. If we took the girls to story time at the library, or one of the "structured playgroups" offered by our town's family net-work, she'd be the kid practically up on the teacher or librarian's lap, eager to be as close to the action as possible. Loud, crowded, overwhelming situations didn't faze her in the least. When we brought the girls to a kids' concert once, in a good-sized theater, she ran up to the edge of the stage and danced her tail off with other kids mostly a year or two older than her. Had she been wearing a bra, she no doubt would have flung it at the bass player.

Clio spent that same concert glued to my lap, and even protested when I tried to "dance" with her there. (The old parental lap dance.) And this is how she'd become, at two years and change, in almost any new and unfamiliar situation. She hung back close to Alastair or me and in some cases wouldn't make eye contact with other people, or would even "freeze": she'd stand completely still wherever she was, focused on the floor or a piece of furniture. As if by staying still and quiet enough, she might disappear completely.

But to see her the way she was when nobody else was around and it was just the four of us, you'd think she'd be the life of the party. She was silly and playful, and loved to be tickled and picked up and spun around. She was a total chatterbox—much more so than her sister. At any given moment she was likely to burst into the ABC song, "Twinkle, Twinkle," or "Happy Birthday."

Sometimes she would warm up, eventually, around new people. But she was never quite the quirky, engaging little nut job she was at home, in her comfort zone. It was a little heartbreaking to see her so frightened, so ill at ease, so much of the time. Still, we were careful not to push her too hard, and instead gently encouraged her to relax, go ahead, try.

I'm sure the dynamic was complicated by the fact that Elsa was always off like a shot, immediately engaging (and sometimes overengaging) with other people and situations. Was Clio intimidated by this, thinking that there was no option to be semi-outgoing, that she had to go all in? Or did she want to differentiate

herself from her sister on some level? Or—a third possibility—
maybe she just liked the chance for some one-on-one cuddle
time with Mom and Dad?

It was sometimes troubling how other people reacted to Clio's
shyness, too. Because Elsa was so charmingly, disarmingly outgoing, Clio's behavior was thrown into sharp relief, and I think—
and know, in a couple of cases—that some people thought there
was something "wrong" with her, mentally or emotionally. Other
people seemed almost offended by the fact that she wouldn't laugh
or smile or chatter with them the way Elsa immediately would.

Once, while Alastair was otherwise occupied, I took the
girls with me to the pharmacy to pick up a few things. While
we waited at the checkout, Elsa smiled and said "hi!" to a sixty-
something woman also waiting in line.

"Well, hello, sweetheart!" she said, in a cootchy-wootchy
sort of voice. "And how old are you?"

"Twoooo!" Elsa said, holding up two fingers. And added,
"I'm Elsa!"

"Hel-*lo,* Elsa! And how old are you?" she said to Clio, who
had been studying the woman, unsmiling, all this time.

Clio did not answer.

"She's also two," I said. "They're twins."

"Oh, well I wouldn't have known," the woman said. She
sounded annoyed. "One talkative one and one quiet one, hm?"

"Well, sometimes they switch, and *she's* the talkative one," I
said with a smile, nodding toward Clio.

"Really?" The woman seemed doubtful. She regarded Clio
over her glasses, and her voice wasn't cootchy-wootchy at all
when she said, "Cat got your tongue today, huh?"

Clio (who really is an excellent judge of character) just glared
at her. And I was glad.

This type of scenario repeated itself over and over again. People would go on about how bright and adorable and fun Elsa was, but about Clio, they'd say only, "Amazing, isn't it, how different twins can be."

No more amazing than it is when any two siblings are very different from one another, I'd think. And hold Clio closer, hating the world for not giving her a chance, for not letting her be who she was on her own terms, for seeing her only as a counterpoint to her sister.

Growing up, I was always at the top of my class. I had near-perfect grades, and teachers tended to like me quite a lot, probably all the more because I wasn't a kiss-ass. My brother, who is extremely smart but not very academically inclined, dreaded having the same teachers that I'd had, knowing that sooner or later they'd realize that he wasn't the student I was and be disappointed. He feared (and in the case of certain teachers, I'm guessing he was justified) that on account of the contrast he'd be viewed as inadequate instead of just different.

And we're three years apart. I suspect this kind of thing— not wanting to be defined in contrast to your sibling—is an even more significant issue with twins. I'm sure there will be times, perhaps much sooner than I think, when my girls ache to be seen on their own terms, as individuals. Not as part of a matched (or intriguingly mismatched) set.

I didn't tell anyone about my new diagnosis immediately. Not even my parents. I didn't want to alarm them, especially my mother, who I knew would immediately think of her sister and worry that I might be headed down that road.

And I wanted to regain equilibrium first. Soon after we added the mood stabilizer to my drug cocktail, the mood swings,

anxiety, and low-grade depression I'd been experiencing dissipated, and I felt better. For a few days the new drug made me
feel sleepy and headachy, and at night I had what felt like hot
flashes—if having the sudden urge to rip off my pajamas and
down a glass of ice water is what a hot flash feels like. But these
side effects didn't last.

I felt calm and more or less content. But I was acutely aware
of the fact that it was contentment of a more subdued nature than
what I'd felt weeks earlier. Which was good, of course. Because
I had, in fact, been too happy. But I had to admit, I missed that
high.

Now, faced with plain and simple reality, as opposed to the
enhanced version, I found myself looking a bit more realistically
and reflectively at my life:

I hadn't written anything new since finishing my novel the
year before, and was still clinging to hope that I'd find a publisher in spite of rapidly waning options. But my grip on that
hope was weakening. And I knew that sooner or later I had to
move on. I had to find the next project.

This would be difficult, though, as I was spending more time
at work, usually working closer to thirty-five hours a week than
the twenty-five I was being paid for. I was being given more
responsibility, too, and invited to participate and present at more
new businesses pitches.

Meanwhile, on the home front, things were intense. On the
one hand, Elsa and Clio were amazing—quickly going from
toddlers of the baby sort to toddlers of the more *kid* sort. They
noticed and experienced the world around them, rather than just
toddling half-obliviously through it. Taking them to a museum
or a petting zoo or even just sitting and coloring with them was
much more fun now. I began to feel infinitely closer to them as

I started to enjoy their company as *people*. Motherhood was start-ing to feel like something more than just taking care of my chil-dren; it had a new dimension now, of actually relating to them. It was the aspect of parenting I had looked forward to ever since they were babies.

As they edged closer to two-and-a-half, their verbal skills were making quantum leaps, too. They were starting to speak in full sentences, conjugate verbs, and add sophisticated new words to their vocabularies: "Stroller." "Sandwich." "Apricot." "Monkey."

The words that held the most thrall for them were, naturally, of the scatological variety: "poop," "poo-poo," "pee-pee," "bum-bum," "toot" (=flatulence), "yoni" (our chosen term for girl parts, for its ability to encompass both vulva and vagina). Stuffed animals and dolls were christened "Poop" and "Pee-pee," as was pretty much everything else, anthropomorphizing household ob-jects being a big hit at that time. E.g., Clio holds up her sippy cup and says, in a falsetto voice, "My name is poo poo!" and Elsa holds up hers and says, "My name is pee-pee!" (Look out Har-vard, here we come!)

They liked to talk about actual poop, too. One spring day, as they were waking up from their afternoon nap, I overheard the following crib-to-crib exchange:

Elsa: (excited) I making a big poopie, Kee-o
Clio: (no response)
Elsa: (even more excited) I make a BIG poopie, Kee-o!
Clio: (conciliatory) That's OK, Elsa.

So it was, in many ways, a golden age of cuteness. But at the same time—man, were they a challenge. The tantrums, the testing, the willfulness, and the whining were all ramping steadily up.

It was around this time that Clio began having some particularly challenging behavioral issues. Most toddlers are obsessive-compulsive to a degree. But with Clio, it had become much more than just wanting the blue sippy cup instead of the pink or wanting to sit on the left side in the car, instead of the right. It was wanting reality to conform precisely to whatever vision she had in her small head of the way things ought to be.

So, if Clio made a statement, such as, "After library we go back to we house" and we answered her with, "Yep, that's right" when she actually wanted us to say, "OK," then woe to us. She would scream, hysterically, "No, don't say it! Don't say that!" and then repeat her statement again, through sobs. We would try a different turn of phrase. We tried parroting back what she said. ("Yes, after the library we'll go back to our house.") We tried saying nothing. Sometimes we'd hit on the right answer. Most of the time we didn't.

And once Clio was in screaming mode, there was little we could do to bring her back. The more we said, the harder she screamed. We put her on "time outs" constantly, but she could scream for forty-five minutes or more, nothing doing. We tried yelling. We tried hugging and comforting her, breathing deeply in and out as we held her, but nine times out of ten, she'd just stiffen and writhe away, the same way she had as an infant.

It was around this time that I also started consulting some parenting books. The kind by "experts" who promise stronger families, everlasting domestic harmony, and world peace if you just follow their simple, surefire advice.

The problem with these books is that they're written on the assumption that there is only one child losing his or her shit at any given time. And that you, the parent, are able to drop everything and devote your full attention to that shit-losing child.

Nevertheless, they did offer up some tools that seemed worth adding to our parenting belts.

One book I read recommended speaking "Toddlerese": basically, talking to toddlers in their own language and intonation when they're upset or angry. You start by acknowledging what they want or feel, with toddleresque simplicity, to let them know that they are heard and understood; then you shift into what you'd like them to do.

I tried it for the first time one morning that April. The four of us were in the car on the way to a farm with a petting zoo, and Clio was loudly and angrily demanding to go to the playground instead. I said something along the lines of, "Playground! Playground! You want to go to the playground! You want to go now! Playgrounds are fun! And we'll go to the playground later! But now we're going to the farm to see some animals. And it will be fun, too! But now you need to calm down."

Alastair looked at me like I was demented. I'd told him about this notion of mirroring back the children's feelings before saying "no" or making a contrary demand, but I hadn't exactly mentioned the Toddlerese part.

"Wait a second," he said. "You're supposed to talk like them, too? That doesn't seem right."

Honestly, that had been my initial thought, too. It did seem almost too accommodating in some way, this relinquishing of your adult dignity for the sake of your child. Then again, trying to reason calmly in grammatical English with a screaming two-year-old isn't the most dignified activity either.

Clio, like her father, initially looked at me like I was deranged. She was silent for a few, shocked seconds, which was nice. But then she resumed yelling, "I just want to go to dee play-ground!" Shortly thereafter Elsa, who'd apparently had enough of the screaming, began to cry. (I can't say I blamed her. I was on the verge myself.) And now we had two unhappy and very loud toddlers in our backseat.

They were so loud and unhappy, and we were so unable to quiet them—either through Toddlerese or calm Parentese or even very loud, end-of-our rope Parentese—that finally we just stopped talking to them altogether. "We're not going to talk to you when you're crying and yelling," we said several self-contradictory times.

They kept crying and yelling.

Until Alastair tried a classic parenting maneuver: he pulled the car over to the side of the road. We both got out. And stood there, waiting for the girls to calm down. Whether out of compliance or complete bewilderment, they did.

Thus proving that while newfangled, developmentally appropriate approaches to managing your children certainly can be helpful, sometimes your parents and grandparents really did know best.

Most of the time, thank the good Lord in heaven, the girls didn't have all-out screaming fits at the same time. But this came with its own concern: we sometimes felt like we were neglecting Elsa in order to focus on her sister. There are times when I even found myself pleading sternly with her as if she were a few years, as opposed to a few minutes, older. "Come on, Elsa, be a big girl and stop whining for a minute, please. Clio is upset and I have to deal with her. You can see that." As if it was her responsibility to be the "good one," for our and her sister's sake.

I came to hate the days, or stretches of days, when one of the girls—and it certainly wasn't always Clio—was making me crazy while the other one wasn't. I still hate those days. And, strange as it may sound, I hate them even more than the days when *both* of the girls are driving me crazy. Because on the lopsided days, when it's a struggle to be evenhanded in the amount of attention or patience I'm giving my daughters, I am forced to acknowledge my fear—as small but as sharp as the finest needle—that maybe, deep down, I love one of the them more than the other.

I wonder: Am I being too hard on the "problem" child—harder than I would be if her sister were behaving the same way? Or am I letting her off the hook too easily? Am I more patient with one than the other in general? When there are fights, do I rule in one's favor more often than in the other's?

The irony is that I actually have the "maybe I love you more . . ." fear about both of the girls, depending on the day or the week. I should take some comfort in that, I suppose.

I'd be far more comfortable, though, if the thought never even crossed my mind.

So, was I happy with my life circumstances around this time, between work and life and the terrible twos? I guess you could say yes and no.

But at least I didn't feel unrealistically happy anymore, nor did I feel depressed. And that was nice. While it lasted.

Unfortunately, by early May—about six weeks after I'd started the new medication—the sands of my mood were starting to shift again, and quickly. I'd go from feeling irritable to anxious to weepy to giggly to downright depressed within the space of days or even hours.

Sometimes my quickness to emote felt good and sweet and

poignant: on one of the first truly warm days of spring, while I was out in the backyard with the girls, starting to get our tiny vegetable garden ready for planting, Elsa crouched next to me, intently watching a worm wriggle through a clump of dirt: "A leetle worm!" she said in a high, squeaky voice. "I love him!"

And I welled up with tears, utterly delighted and grateful for the gift of Elsa, Clio, worms, vegetable gardens, everything. At the same time, I had a melancholy sense that I was on the verge of losing it all.

And then I *would* lose it: some small, hard-to-swallow event would trigger magnified anger and disappointment (in the case of a much-loved coworker being rather abruptly and unfairly laid off) or a disproportionate surge of jealousy followed by depression (a friend selling her novel for six figures in a matter of days). Meanwhile, my patience was paper-thin when it came to dealing with the girls. I snapped and yelled at them far more than I would have liked.

I was an emotional seismograph. The tiniest tremor sent that needle a shakin'.

But it wasn't all bad: my old pal hypomania came back to visit me a few times, too. Once, I came home from an exuberant night out at a writing event and told Alastair that I knew it sounded weird, but I really, truly felt like everybody there loved me. It was like they were sort of magnetically drawn to me.

A lesser man would have said I was being an asshole, but Alastair pointed out that maybe, just maybe, could I be feeling the tiniest bit, um, elevated?

Another time, I was invited to participate in a seminar at work and was convinced I was the smartest person in the room, so full was I of sparkling insights, observations, and wit. At the same time, I worried I was coming across as an overbearing narcissist and worked hard to restrain myself from saying everything that came to mind. (But everything I had to say was so *good*!) The moderator himself pulled me aside afterward to say, admiringly, and with sincerity, "Wow, you're a rock star, aren't you?"

I sure as hell felt like one. Except, of course, when I didn't.

Around this time, my doctor decided to further reduce the amount of antidepressant I was taking, concerned that it was causing the volatility, and to ratchet up the mood stabilizer. Meanwhile, I decided I could use another health care player on Team Jane.

I've never felt much need for therapy. In high school when I was having some issues with food and weight and wanting to be—and succeeding in being—really skinny, I saw one of the school's counselors a few times. He wasn't much help, and I grew out of my unhealthy relationship with food on my own, gradually, over the next several years.

Once, when I was in my midtwenties, having a bit of a quarter-life crisis about my career direction—and, oh yes, on an experimental "break" from the antidepressants I'd started a couple of years earlier—I saw a therapist for a few months. She was a good sounding board as I puzzled through my emerging realization that advertising copywriting wasn't destined to be my passion, just my job, and that (non-advertising) writing was where my heart was leading me. There were a few issues with my family that she provided some insights into as well. But the best piece of advice she gave me? I should probably get back on antidepressants.

Since then, I'd never felt the need to "talk to someone" as the euphemism goes. I didn't—and still don't—feel as if I had any deep-seated, problematic issues with self-esteem or interpersonal relationships or existential angst.

But that spring, I felt like I needed *something*. Not therapy, exactly, but someone who could help me cope with my symptoms and better understand the triggers—stress, writerly angst, screaming children, etc.—that exacerbated them.

I managed to find a psychologist who specialized in bipolar disorder, and who turned out to be exactly what I needed. He was a tall, soft-spoken man with a sweet smile, a twinkle in his eye, and, yes, a beard (albeit a small, chin-only, Abraham Lincoln–esque one). He taught me a great deal about the manifestations and chemistry of bipolar. I liked this: having concrete knowledge of what was going on behind the scenes, so to speak. I also liked the list he gave me of famous people with bipolar disorder. (Oh, Axl Rose. I always did feel like you and I had a special connection . . .)

And while I never went down the family dynamics and interpersonal relationships rabbit hole with this doctor, since neither of us deemed it necessary, I did open up about the fact that I'd always been a high achiever and, as such, was dismayed by this feeling that my best pal, my brain, had turned on me. I hated this feeling that my rational and emotional reactions had somehow fallen out of calibration: I couldn't gauge what was truly upsetting / stressful / hurtful / important and what only appeared that way through the distorted lens of depression. In the past, it had always been much clearer to me.

Being able to talk about all this with a therapist was a relief. It was good to have a touchstone—someone on solid ground to help me put things in perspective. But it didn't make the bad days easier.

And it didn't help me feel any better about what a shitty mother I was being—or felt like I was being much of the time, anyway.

I just didn't have the emotional reserves to deal calmly and patiently with the girls, and found myself snapping at them, yelling at them, even handling them more roughly than I should have when battling with them to get dressed or undressed (what *is* it with toddlers and clothes?) or into their car seats mid-tantrum.

And then I'd feel guilty and terrible, pull myself together, and promise—swear up and down—that I was going to be more calm and patient and understanding. (These were my *babies*. My beloved, beloved girls!) And when I was feeling good, I could pull it off—do the whole strategic empathy thing: *Wow, you seem really mad! It's no fun to get dressed when you'd rather play, is it? But it's time to go, and that means we need to get dressed.*

But then they'd press and test, and one would be whining and tugging on me while I was trying to be lovingly firm with the screaming other one, and I'd snap—in seconds, I went from their smiling, patient, playful mom to monster mom, fighting back the urge to smack them. Other times, I'd just find myself yelling, pleading, "Please! Will you just STOP? Can't you see I'm trying to help, here??"

I could see the bewilderment in their eyes when my mood turned on a dime. I knew that my volatility wasn't good for them—or fair to them. I hated that I wasn't strong enough to keep my mood swings in check when I was around my girls. I hated that my depression had become a fifth member of our family.

My depression was largely to blame for the shortness of my twin-wrangling fuse, no doubt. But not completely. I suspect that many parents of two-year-olds—twin and otherwise—feel at times exactly how I felt, regardless of their mental health: utterly frustrated and powerless.

A friend of mine who has twins roughly the same age as I do recommended a series of books about child development.

"It's old, and very seventies," she warned me, "but a lot of it still rings true."

The key takeaway for her was the authors' assertion that kids more or less fall apart around the half-year mark, at any age. My friend found this comforting, in a perverse sort of way, her twins having just passed the two-and-a-half-year mark. With my girls nearing that milestone, she thought that I might, too.

I did. It was comical, actually: after expounding on the delights of two-year-olds in the first half of the book—how curious and playful they are, eager to explore their world, but still affectionate and sweet!—the authors basically kick off the second half by advising Mother (it was the seventies, remember) to arrange some extra help from family, friends, or babysitters as their child approached two-and-a-half. And that's on the assumption that mother has only *one* two-and-a-half-year-old child.

But although there were times during this period when I felt like I wanted to spend as little time as possible with the girls, and even kind of, well, disliked them—who knew I was capable of this?—I still *loved* them fiercely. And more often than not, I actually liked them, too. Between the mental maelstroms that left me too drained and impatient and depressed to focus on anything besides my own emotions and the tantrums and whining that left me feeling even more frazzled and fragile, there were moments of crystalline joy and downright fun.

The same Clio who would scream relentlessly if I put her left sock on before her right one and refused to take them off and start over would, later the same day, be riding with me in the cart at Target and, passing a rack of bras, say in her little helium voice, "Look, Mommy! Magic hats!" making me want to scoop her up and devour her right then and there.

And the same Elsa who would body slam her sister intentionally, twice, or fling her food to the floor with a baiting, mischievous glint in her eye, then wail with operatic tragedy when removed from the scene or denied dessert, would also spontaneously engulf us in bear hugs or grab her sister's hands, giggling, for a game of ring around the rosy, turning my heart to Play-Doh.

I began to feel more acutely aware of the fact that this phase of preschool sweetness, when our girls were still fully "ours," both in hours and needs, was fleeting. And a growing part of me wished I could be a bigger part of my girls' lives on a daily basis.

So, it's rather insane what I did that June.

Not long after that seminar wherein I was a complete rock star, I decided that in order to fulfill my rock star destiny—not to mention get paid for the hours I was regularly working above and beyond my allotted twenty-five and be able to take on the added responsibilities being thrown my way—I should officially go up to thirty-five hours a week at work. My writing wasn't going anywhere, and I wasn't doing much of it anyway. I'd still have Fridays with the girls. I'd put the extra money in savings, and in a couple of years, when the girls were in kindergarten, I'd quit and finally go freelance.

This was a stupid decision. I almost immediately regretted it. Now, instead of being something I did in order to support my writing and allow me some time to be with my children, my job felt like it was defining me. And although the extra money was helpful, we'd been getting by fine without it. Anyway, how lucky had I been to be able to work part-time, when so many women don't have that choice?

I probably should have listened to my psychologist, who advised me not to make any major decisions for a while. Rocking the boat wasn't a good idea for someone whose brain was being rocked by a chemical imbalance. Moreover, I probably didn't have the clarity and perspective to accurately evaluate the ramifications of a big life choice.

But if I hadn't made that stupid decision, I might not have hit rock bottom several months later. And I might not have made (ignoring my psychologist's advice yet again) one of the best decisions of my life.

20

I don't do well with heat and humidity. I loathe it, really. My hands and feet get swollen and I feel sluggish and fat and unmotivated—even when I'm *not* depressed. I blame my Anglo-Saxon ancestors for this. I also blame them for the fact that I'm too cheap and self-flagellating to put air conditioners anywhere in our house but our and the girls' bedrooms.

One sweltering Saturday in August, I was dying to escape the heat (our house, my life) somehow. Flying to Iceland might have been a nice way to do this, but taking a drive somewhere seemed a more practical alternative. I tried to channel my old pre-kids weekend-drive spirit, pulled out a map of Massachusetts, and looked for someplace the four of us could go that wouldn't be too far (e.g., Iceland) or too crowded (e.g., anything within five miles of the ocean).

There was a large body of water, a reservoir, about forty minutes' drive due west, which I was pretty sure I'd been to before.

I vaguely remembered a picnic area or a park along one side of it. This seemed perfect: we could enjoy a nice, air-conditioned ride, then pop out for a quick picnic. Maybe we'd find a place to get ice cream, too. Forty-five minutes each way was pushing it for a day trip, but with any luck the girls would sleep at least one way.

So we packed up the diaper bag, got everyone into the car, cranked the tunes and the AC, and headed on our way.

My mood was not good. I didn't feel depressed to the point of immobilization, but I did, on that particular day, have the strange sensation that I'd gotten lost somewhere along the way—that the life I was living wasn't quite my own. I hoped that getting away would give me a bit of perspective and lift my spirits, at least temporarily.

And at first things looked promising. The drive was pretty. The girls were chatty and cheerful. We stopped at a farm-stand-type grocery store to get some sandwiches—that is, Alastair got the sandwiches while I chased around after the girls and tried to keep them from grabbing and eating any of the apples for sale, all appealingly displayed and seemingly there for the taking. To distract the girls, I decided to let them each pick out an old-fashioned candy stick. Perfect idea. They were immediately very, very excited. But while I was at the register paying, Clio started to pull a bag of something or other off a rack, and the cashier said to her—firmly but gently and completely appropriately—"No no, hon, that's not for you."

Clio froze. She looked down at the floor. And then her mouth started to pull down at the corners. She began to tremble. And suddenly—kapow! She began screaming, loudly and repeatedly, *"I want my ga-ga!"* while tears streamed down her cheeks.

The cashier looked at her in shock and said, defensively, "Sorry, did I do something wrong?"

I assured her that she hadn't, quickly scooped Clio up, signaled frantically to Alastair, still back at the deli counter, to come get Elsa, and went outside, trying to soothe Clio while simultaneously cursing myself: I'd forgotten to pack the girls' ga-gas.

Long story short: Clio screamed nonstop for the next hour and a half. The reservoir didn't actually have any sort of picnic area anywhere near it, and we ended up sitting in a patch of thistly grass on the side of the road, where we were devoured by mosquitoes. The sandwiches were awful. There was a hot, hard breeze, and the napkins kept blowing away. Clio kept crying. And on the drive home, Elsa joined her.

When we got home, we put them into their cribs, where they fell asleep within minutes.

I went back downstairs for a glass of ice water, and out our kitchen window saw that a tree-removal crew had started to dismember the big old oak tree in the yard directly behind ours— the only big tree in our neighborhood, and one that had provided shade for our yard. I used to hold the girls up to look at it when they were babies: *See the birdies? Look at all those birdies?* Most of its limbs were already gone.

I started to cry. I went back upstairs and got into bed next to Alastair, who had lain down for a nap. "Our life," I said, through tears, "is so small."

"What does that mean?" he said, hurt. He was worn down at that point by my steadily worsening mood swings, temper, and general malaise.

"I don't know," I said. "Our house, our neighborhood, my job, the girls. And the tree. They're taking down the tree." The chainsaws were roaring outside as I spoke.

"What about us? Are you unhappy with us?"

"No. Of course not, baby. I just . . . I don't know."

"This is depression talking. Look, I need to sleep. Let's just try to sleep, OK?"

I told him I loved him.

He said he loved me, too, then added, "I miss you."

"I do too," I said. "I'm sorry."

At the tail end of August, we spent a week at a family camp in New Hampshire, as we've done for years—and as Alastair has, with his parents, since he was four or five years old. It's a world unto itself, on an island on Lake Winnipesaukee, where families come and live in cabins, eat meals together in a dining hall, and spend their days canoeing or swimming or reading by the water, playing tennis and bocce, doing craft projects, and otherwise enjoying "grown-up" camp. There are activities for the kids. And a lot of cocktail parties, too.

Every year we go, I'm amazed that it's been a whole year since we were there last. Everything—the root-studded paths, the smell of the lake water, the smooth, weathered wood of the Adirondack chairs by the waterfront—is so familiar, so unchanging. The sensation must be even more poignant for Alastair and his parents, who are among the families with the longest tenure.

The only thing that felt notably different this year was the fact that the girls, no longer babies, could now experience the island in new ways. There were things we could actually *do* with them—play on the little climbing structure and slide, take walks, build sand castles on the beach—as opposed to just following them around and redirecting them when they were about to toddle, suicidally, into the lake. Elsa proved herself to be a dancing fiend, trying valiantly to keep up with the "big kids" (i.e., the five- and six-year-olds) at the family dances, and joined me for some yoga on the ball field one morning. The girls and I also came up with our own version of bocce: you run up and down the court with your hands over your head, yelling "bocce bocce bocce!" Everybody wins.

So there were plenty of lovely moments. But my mood was still shaky. My doctor had recently added a second mood stabilizer to my cocktail, which was supposed to give my mood a bump but thus far didn't appear to be giving me anything except pimples.

Meanwhile, I was feeling increasingly miserable about my new, more full-time work schedule. I had been so, so fortunate to be able to work part-time, and was furious with myself for having stupidly gone and put my thumb on the scale, throwing everything out of balance.

I'd felt it most keenly one evening after work when I went to meet Alastair and the girls plus several of our friends with kids at a kids' concert at a park by a pond near us. As I arrived—in my work clothes, straight from a day of sitting at my desk inside the dark agency office—the girls, in bathing suits, their feet sandy, ran to me, arms outstretched, yelling "Mommy! Mommy!" And it was all I could do not to break down crying in front of our friends and acquaintances.

I tried to act normally, to smile and banter with our friends, push the girls on the swings, and enjoy the warm evening, but my heart wouldn't stop racing, and the tears wouldn't stop coming, and my insides hurt. I found myself quite literally doubled over, on the beach, trying to get a hold of myself, begging with Clio, who'd run after me and was asking (well, telling) me to come push her on the swings, to please just go back to Daddy, please, I needed some space. Please, please, please. I'm sorry, I'm sorry, I'm sorry.

There had been several episodes like this throughout the summer—panic-attack-like in their intensity. I had one or two less severe episodes while we were at the camp, too. Still, I was on a beautiful island, away from my everyday life, and somehow it all felt a little safer. I began to dread going back home—back to feeling trapped at work, back to thinking I was feeling better and then realizing (piling frustration and sadness onto depression) that I wasn't.

Coming back was all of that and worse. Much, much worse.

Which is why, at the girls' nursery school orientation a couple of weeks later, I was a complete mess.

At two years, eight months, and change, the girls were just old enough to sneak in under the wire and start preschool. Our search for a school the previous winter had been a brief one, given that we couldn't afford most of the options near us. Even with sibling discounts, the cost of sending both of the girls to one of the earthy-crunchy, progressive, organic-paints, and teachers-with-masters-degrees schools that proliferate in the Greater Boston area would have been prohibitive. But we managed to find a very nice little school where we could send the girls a couple of mornings a week without having to refinance our house.

I was excited for them. I knew they were ready to add some structured time to their routine, kick their social skills up a notch, and expand their sphere of comfort beyond our living room. I was confident that Elsa would take to it like a duck to water. We knew it might take a bit longer for Clio but weren't worried.

I had always adored the anticipation and cozy thrill of back-to-school time, and now I got to live it vicariously through my daughters for the next twenty-odd years. I couldn't wait for all the preschool rituals and experiences ahead: the coat hooks and cubbies with their names on them and the craft projects brought proudly home (flash forward to our house six months later, every surface cluttered with those damned, adorable craft projects—piles and piles of them, crusty with dried paint and glue and shedding glitter—and me trying to figure out how to sneak some of them into the recycling bin without the girls catching on . . .).

Was I feeling torn or sad about the whole thing—my little babies, leaving the nest and becoming preschoolers? Sure, definitely. It was a big step. But there was a lot more than that going on in my turbulent little brain the day we brought the girls and ourselves in for the open house a few days before school started.

Hence the reason I was fighting back tears, and sometimes losing the battle, almost the whole time we were there. I don't know what was more painful: hearing Clio crying as we left her in the classroom and went down the hall with the other parents to learn about school procedures or having to say no when Elsa asked if I was going to bring her back again.

That is, I told her yes, she would come back in a few days to start school. But no, Daddy would be bringing her. Except on rare occasions, I wouldn't be the one to bring the girls to school and help them hang their coats up on the little hooks, or be the one to ooh and ahh over their craft projects as they handed them to me at the end of the day. That would be Daddy. I'd be at work.

But neither of these things, in and of themselves, was what felt so achingly awful. It was these things compounded by the underlying feeling that my depression was causing me to miss out on my children. Mentally, emotionally, I simply wasn't fully there. I was looking up at my world and myself from somewhere far down below it, trying—longing—to climb back up to it. But every time I thought I was getting close, I'd tumble back down the hill. And there I'd be, down at the bottom again.

My work weeks fell into a similarly Sisyphean pattern: I'd feel utterly miserable, tearful, and despondent on Mondays; worse on Tuesdays; and a little better by Wednesday afternoons. Thursdays were bearable to good, and Fridays, my day off, better. By Saturday and Sunday I felt almost normal, and couldn't believe I'd felt so horrific the week before. I was quite sure that things were on the upswing. But Monday morning, it was rinse and repeat.

Several times, I played hooky or went home early on Mondays and Tuesdays, simply unable to stomach the weight and ache of the depression in my body. Unable to keep up the charade of normalcy. I pled headache and stomach bug and babysitter crisis. Nobody blinked.

Throughout it, somehow, I still managed to keep getting my work done—though probably not as well or as creatively as I ought to have. But advertising is all about appearances, and I think I took a perverse and bitter sort of pleasure in making everything look shiny and bright on the surface. In my mind, my descriptions of innovative solutions and groundbreaking innovations were dripping with sarcasm. But to the rest of the world they just looked like damned good copy.

Suddenly I couldn't bear the thought of coming into this place four days a week for three more years. But *why* was work making me so unhappy? I liked what I did; I was very fond of the people. Yes, I wished I was only working three days, not my new four, but could an extra eight hours really, truly, have plunged me into such depths?

I kept trying to get it back, to rediscover the contentment I'd felt for the previous four years—as if it were just hidden somewhere. Stuck in the back of the supply cabinet or in a corner underneath my desk. If I could just find it and shake the dust off of it, I'd be fine. But I couldn't find it, no matter how hard I looked.

It was the depression, I tried to tell myself. The depression, the depression, the depression—throwing its shadow over everything, addling my brain and obscuring the big picture. As soon as I felt better (when?), work would feel better, too.

I thought very seriously about taking medical leave. Alastair urged me to talk to my supervisor or to the head of Human Resources and be frank with them about what was going on—ask if, at the very least, they could delegate some of my work for a while, until I was better. Or, he suggested, what about just asking to revert back to a three-day-a-week schedule? Maybe that would help me get back to the right balance.

My psychologist had similar suggestions. And they were all very reasonable. But even just contemplating them sent me into paroxysms of anxiety and woe. The powers that be at work wouldn't really "get it"—they couldn't possibly understand clinical depression. I didn't want everyone knowing I had this problem—capable, rock star me. And what about the professional repercussions? What if I was forever branded as "unstable"? God knows it wouldn't help my case if I did end up going freelance and word got out that I was a breakdown waiting to happen.

And if I asked to go back to three days? What kind of loopy, wishy-washy, entitled pain in the ass would I look like if I did that? The management was already being generously accommodating to let me work part-time—nobody else at the company did. How could I go back and ask them for something *else*?

As for leaving to freelance—which was what, in my heart of hearts, I suspected was the solution—the thought of it was terrifying. Could I take that kind of risk as the primary breadwinner for our family? And as someone with major depression? Not to mention the fact that there was a recession on.

So for the moment, I was stuck.

21

One evening in early October, when I walked in the door after work, the girls greeted me at the door, crying jubilantly, "Hear this, Mommy! Hear this!"

They launched into a song they were learning at school for their Halloween show: "I'm a wittle punkin, short and stout. Here are my eyes, and here is my mouth. When it's Halloween and you are out, just lift my lid and I will shout: Boo!"

It was a Tuesday evening, and therefore my mood was at its weekly nadir. I had barely made it through the workday. But now I summoned a smile and clapped. "Wow! That was *great* girls!"

The girls' smiles turned immediately to glares. "Noooo!!" they cried.

"What's the matter?"

"You're supposed to be scared and say 'aah!'" Alastair instructed from the living room.

"Oh," I said, my heart falling just a little bit. He knew what to do; I didn't. He had probably heard the song multiple times since noon that day, when he had picked the girls up from pre-school. And the repetition was probably starting to gnaw at his sanity. But I would have taken that kind of annoyance over being at my desk at work all day, feeling wretched and trapped. "Do it again, girls," I said. "Please?"

They sang the song again (such precious pronunciation: "wittle punkin"), and this time I screamed in mock fright at the end. The girls were completely satisfied with my performance.

Just like the rest of the world was.

I was limping my way through it all: work, errands, even social interactions to some degree. While inside, I felt darker and deader than I ever had in my life.

The girls were adjusting beautifully to their two mornings per week at preschool and seemed to really enjoy the things they were doing and learning—the punkin song, for one.

Clio cried at drop-off and reportedly stuck very close to the teachers for the first two or three days, but gradually got more comfortable, as she would continue to do over the course of the year. Elsa jumped right in with both feet, but apparently had some "sharing issues," which wasn't surprising to hear.

You'd think that twins would be better at sharing than most kids, given that they have to do it all the time. And if my girls are any indication, then yes: twins share beautifully—exactly fifty percent of the time. The other fifty percent, they fight like sailors.

The disputes at that time tended to fall into five distinct categories: there was the "you took what I was playing with and I want it back" fight; the "you are crowding my personal space" fight; the "I am mad at you for some entirely inane and irrational reason, like you put your milk cup to the left of your plate and I want it to the right of your plate" fight; and the "you are doing some silly/annoying thing on purpose just to drive me nuts" fight. Then there were the expressions-of-affection-and-playfulness-turned-rough incidents, which, while not as contentious, still required parental intervention.

I hated having to play referee. Because Elsa tended to be the more physically dominant one, prone to literally throwing her weight around, I worried that I was too quick to blame her for starting things. On the other hand, Clio tended to get unreasonably upset when Elsa crowded her space or cramped her style, and Clio could be incredibly bossy. I couldn't exactly blame Elsa for getting fed up when Clio tried to dictate the rules of LEGO-castle building ("No! Elmo doesn't want a door on his castle!") or insisted that she and Elsa take turns singing along with their favorite songs, rather than singing together.

Sometimes we tried to leave them to their own devices. "Can you work things out on your own, or do you need help?"

"Need help!" was invariably the answer.

Times when I was feeling particularly exhausted or depressed or simply fed up, I'd think to myself: what would happen if I just ignored them and let them fight it out? Would they tear each other apart—end up bloodied and bruised? Had a fight between two-year-olds ever ended in death? Probably not. But maybe broken bones. Or at least lacerations.

And then it would occur to me that I wasn't being a very good parent, and I'd go in and separate my hysterical children. Stupid questions were asked (by me): "What happened?" "Who started it?" Compromises reached. Time-outs administered. Toys taken away. Apologies forced.

We increasingly looked for ways to stop fighting before it

started. So if there were two of the same toy or doll—which really did make things easier, as much as we hated to go down the two-of-everything road—we wrote the girls' names on them. The girls by that point recognized the letters *E* and *C*. We also used the ABC song trick: you get to play with toy X for as long as it takes Clio to sing the ABC song three times, and then we switch. They weren't crafty enough yet to sing the song at warp speed. We also began to make frequent use of the kitchen timer for these purposes. And it wasn't just for toy sharing: sometimes it was for turns on Mommy's lap, too.

It wouldn't be until almost a year later that we implemented one of the most ingenious twin-conflict-prevention techniques of all, suggested by one of my blog readers: alternating days. It's beautiful in its simplicity: every other day belongs to one kid. So whoever's day it is gets to go first—whether it's for less desirable activities, like getting dressed or brushing teeth (the horror!) or more fun stuff, like picking out their frozen waffle (woo hoo!!) or having their bedtime story read. The twin of the day also gets their choice of things like where in the car to sit, which TV show to watch, and the like. The girls take it very, very seriously. And it works like a charm.

But jeez. Who knew that raising children would be such a tactical exercise? When I used to imagine being a mother—even a mother of toddlers—I think I thought it would all unfold much more naturally and organically. I had no idea I'd feel so frequently stymied by how to manage the million daily disputes. I had no idea there would need to be rules of engagement. And kitchen timers? If I'd known, I might have registered for one along with the receiving blankets and crib sheets. Or a six-pack of them, actually; the girls managed to break at least one, and I've melted two or three on the stove in the course of my adult life.

Sibling rivalry isn't just a twin phenomenon, of course. My brother and I had our share of fights. Once I even gave him a fat lip. But that was when we were older. When I was two-and-a-half, he wasn't born yet. And by the time he was two-and-a-half, I was a sensible kindergartner—far too mature to get into screaming brawls with a toddler. At least not on a many-times-a-day basis, as far as I know.

But that which did not kill the girls' love for each other at that age only made it stronger. Or something like that. As mentioned, frequently the conflicts we had to break up were playful, puppylike wrestling matches or embraces turned unintentionally painful. The girls loved hugging, lying on top of each other, and tumbling around on the floor together.

About six months later, there would be a period of a few weeks when I'd go into their rooms at night to check on them and find them cuddled together in Clio's bed. It was always Clio's bed, and when I asked them about it, Clio explained: "Elsa asks to come in my bed, and I let her."

"You don't ever want to go over to her bed?"

"No, I like my bed. But she likes it over here with me, so I say yes."

And this is what makes all their bickering and brawling tolerable and even inspiring: they forgive and forget so quickly. They love each other so implicitly. As they get older, it will become more complicated, no doubt. They may grow apart—I suspect that at some point they have to, at least for a little while, to establish a stronger sense of themselves as individuals. (I don't disagree with the philosophy of separating twins in elementary school.) But I hope that they come back together. I hope they'll always be able to go to each other and be welcome.

. . .

I don't have any official measurements or documentation on this or anything, but I'm reasonably sure that Elsa and Clio are the loudest children in the universe. Over the years, when I've told people this, they've smiled and said things like "oh ho ho, no, I think mine are!" But they're wrong. I've seen their children. I've heard their children. Their children have played with mine. And, my friends, those children are no Elsa and Clio.

I think it's partly just their nature. They are very verbal kids, and Clio, in particular, has a powerful set of pipes and a proclivity toward shouting instead of speaking. She will make an excellent stock market floor trader someday. But I do believe that the girls' twin-ness is part of the volume equation. They are constantly trying to talk over each other to win our attention and ensure that they get what they want, preferably before their sister does.

So on a typical morning at our house when the girls were just beginning their preschool career, one might have heard something along the lines of:

I WANT WAFFLES!! MAY I PLEASE HAVE WAFFLES PLEASE? MOMMY PLEASE CAN I HAVE SOME MILK? I WANT WAFFLES, PLEEEESE? MILLLLLLK PLEEEE-ASE!!! CAN I HAVE SYRUP ON MY WAFFLES? NO THE BLUE CUP NOT THE PINK ONE! NO CLIO'S IS THE ORANGE ONE! ARE YOU MAKIN' THE WAFFLES? I WANT SYRUP PLEEEEASE? CAN YOU CUT MY WAF-FLE UP? NO NOT THAT WAY! HEY LOOK, MOMMY, THE KITTY WANTS HER BRES-EK! I WANT MORE SYRUP. CAN YOU CUT MY WAFFLE, TOO, PLEASE

MOMMY? NO THAT'S NOT WHAT I SAID!! THANK
YOU!! THANK YOU!! MAY I HAVE MORE MILK
PLEASE? MOMMY, I SAID THANK YOU!! NOW YOU
SAY "YOU'RE WELCOME." SAY "YOU'RE WEL-
COME"! I WANT MORE WAFFLES!!!

And there I'd be, whirling around the kitchen, feeling like
Rosie, the housekeeper-robot on *The Jetsons,* about to start smoking from my ears and dropping parts on the floor. At the same
time, I'd be trying, frantically, to get the girls to pipe down. Usually I'd start by keeping my voice very quiet and calm, on the
theory that they would have to hush in order to hear me. But this
rarely if ever worked due to the simple fact that they weren't interested in hearing *me.* They wanted to be sure that I heard *them.*
So I'd usually end up screaming over them instead: "I CAN'T
UNDERSTAND YOU WHEN YOU BOTH TALK AT ONCE!" or
"I'M NOT GETTING YOU ANYTHING UNTIL YOU STOP
YELLING!" or "I CAN'T LIVE LIKE THIS!!"

Other times, I just left the room. Walked right out. Which
usually stunned them into silence for a few seconds, and I could
get a few words in before they resumed yelling again.

Between the loud talking and the loud tantrums, you could
say it was a very loud era in our lives. I don't know how we would
have managed if we lived in an apartment or condo with neighbors close by. That is, I don't know how the neighbors would
have managed.

And when we ventured out with the girls, noise management was an important consideration. Particularly when it came
to restaurants. We weren't foolhardy or wealthy enough to eat
out with the girls on a regular basis. But there were a few times
when we had to—while traveling, for example. And there were

other times when we just wanted to get out of the house, rejoin society for an hour or so, and attempt to convince ourselves that maybe, just maybe, we were over the hump and could resume doing some of the things we used to enjoy before the girls were born, this time as a family.

Usually we returned from these outings vowing we'd never eat out with the girls again until they were at least twenty-six. But sometimes, every once in a while, it worked. Like the time we did the before-six early-bird special at a cavernous restaurant / music club / bar. We were the only people there except for the regulars at the bar, so there was no one to object when Elsa informed us, at the top of her lungs, that she LIKED CUCUMBERS!! or to give us dirty looks when Clio started screaming because Elsa took her cucumber (not that she was going to eat it anyway).

Another successful restaurant outing was when we brought the girls along with us to one of Alastair's gigs, a show from 5:00 to 7:00 P.M. at a neighborhood bar—the same one, in fact, that we had escaped to nine months earlier on that particularly exhausting winter's day. Almost nobody was there this time, which, while not the greatest thing for Alastair, was perfect where the girls were concerned. The tall stools at the high-top tables freaked them out at first, but as soon as the french fries showed up, all was well. Ten minutes later they were dancing up a storm to their dad's music, spinning around and careening into barstools like tiny drunks, giggling. A few of the regulars, happily buzzed but not yet soused, smiled fondly in our direction. At one point party-girl Elsa paused mid-dancing to say, "I'm so excited to be here!"

When I took the girls home, a little after six, I felt like I'd actually had a bit of a night out, instead of feeling like I needed a nap to recover. I guess if you're brave and desperate enough to attempt a meal out with loud twin toddlers, there's no place like a dive bar at around five o'clock.

Kids. They grow up so fast. One day they're hanging out in bars, and the next day they're learning how to pee in the toilet.

We'd been meaning all summer long to start potty training the girls. I'd read a book that was recommended to me by my Mothers of Twins Club about a cold-turkey approach that supposedly got great results. But you had to find a three-day block of time where you could hole up inside your house and get the job done. For whatever reason—out-of-town trips, Alastair's gigs, social events, etc.—we had to keep putting it off.

Finally, we settled on Columbus Day weekend for potty boot camp. Or Operation Underpants, as I preferred to call it. It was a weekend, which meant that my mood, in its oscillating state, would be on the happier end of the spectrum—an important consideration: we'd heard from some friends of ours who used this approach that it was surprisingly emotionally exhausting. In addition to wet: "Roll up your rugs," they said, "and make sure you've got a *lot* of underwear on hand."

I bought four twelve-packs from Hanes, which sounds like an insane amount, but which was actually just about right. Other necessary equipment: two potty chairs (purchased months earlier but rarely used), mass quantities of juice and water (the goal was to get them to pee frequently, for more opportunities to "practice"), salty snacks (to keep them drinking—just like in a bar), and dried fruit (to, you know, keep things moving), as well as stickers, treats, and other small rewards for when they made it to the potty in time. Plus lots and lots of old towels and a mop.

The basic idea was to watch the girls—constantly—for signs

that they had to go to the bathroom (wriggling, pacing, etc.) and then escort them there. We had to repeatedly say, "tell me when you need to pee, and we'll go to the potty" and (when applicable) "great job keeping your underwear dry—what a big girl!" And when they managed to do their business in the potty, we showered them with absurd amounts of praise and gave them a sticker or other treat. When they had an accident, we said things along the lines of, "Pee-pee goes in the potty. Next time, when you feel like you need to go, you need to sit on the potty, OK?" And we had to say it in a very calm and nonjudgmental manner. Which is a total piece of cake when you've been cooped up for forty-eight hours with two two-year-olds in a house that smells like an old folks' home and you may or may not be standing in a puddle of urine.

Yes, there was a lot of pee on the floors that weekend, my friends. Many soaked and several soiled pairs of underwear (Elsa was terrified to go #2 in the potty, and would be for several months to come). I myself went through two pairs of jeans and at least two pairs of socks. And on day two, we really did hit the wall: we were physically and emotionally exhausted.

We also made the somewhat rash decision to disassemble the girls' cribs, as a result of our extremely ambitious attempt to night-time potty train them at the same time, so they could get up to use the bathroom on their own when they needed to. This threw me for a complete emotional loop: literally overnight, my babies, who'd slept in cribs and whose diapers I'd changed for the previous 2.9 years, had become little girls who wore underpants and slept in beds. Well, on the floor, that is. We hadn't bought toddler or twin beds ahead of time, so we simply put the crib mattresses on the floor in their room.

Seeing the mattresses there (how sloppy and slovenly they

looked—crack-den-like!—compared to how they had looked in the lovely, contained cribs), I felt a keen, sharp sense of loss. I was suddenly disoriented and out of sorts, and cried quite a bit.

As always: a reasonable enough response to an emotionally intense situation? Sure. Absolutely. But a little exaggerated by my less-than-optimal brain chemistry? Yup.

Alastair and I watched a couple of episodes of *The Daily Show*, which always has a mitigating effect on my mood, or at least distracts me from it. Half-hour doses of televised comedy are the best medicine, after pharmaceuticals.

Alastair had thought from the start that it was crazy to try to potty train the girls *and* attempt to train them overnight, too. He pointed out various spelling errors and inconsistencies in the book we were using as proof that the author was, in fact, insane. He reminded me that the book was not written with twins in mind. He noted that pumping the children full of liquids during the day and then expecting them not to pee all night seemed like a recipe for disaster. And he argued that waking the girls up an hour earlier than normal so they could pee, as the book advised, seemed unnecessarily cruel—to us, that is. On this point, I agreed. But have I mentioned I'm something of an overachiever? And it did seem logically sound that if you were going to teach your children not to pee in their pants during the day, it was strange to change those expectations at night.

So we tried. For three nights. Three dreadful nights, during which Clio—who was apparently terrified at the prospect of wetting her bed—was awake between three and six in the morning and calling every ten minutes for us: "I need to make pee pee!" We tried ignoring her, but eventually she would be up yelling for so long that she actually *did* need to go.

After the third night, we realized that we'd made a mistake. We went out and bought several large packages of pull-ups. We didn't reassemble the cribs, although a part of me would have liked to. Instead, we bought a couple of toddler beds. And once those were assembled and I could tuck my babies back into a nice, contained sleeping space, complete with bed rail, I felt much less wistful. Although I soon started feeling a different kind of wistful—more like mournful, I guess—when we had to go through the nightly battle of getting the girls to stay *in* their new toddler beds.

As for the outcome of Operation Underpants as far as daytime training was concerned? An unqualified success. Of course, there would be many accidents in the days to come. Getting Elsa to overcome her fear of poop would continue to be a challenge over the next several months, and even beyond. And there would be occasional periods of regression and backsliding. But we never went back to diapers. Shortly after the girls' third birthday, we dispensed with pull-ups at bedtime, too. Transition accomplished.

Not to toot my or my husband's own horns, but we were pretty proud of ourselves for this accomplishment. I mean, double, simultaneous potty training? Pretty hardcore. We earned ourselves a few classic expressions of singleton-parent awe/relief over that one: "How do you do it?" "I can't imagine." "It's hard enough with one."

Of course, the answer to all of these questions—in any context—is that raising twins is not a matter of being some kind of superhuman wonder parent. We simply don't have a choice. We just do it. (Anyone at Nike reading this? I'm a size small. Yoga pants, shorts, and some tank tops would be great.) Not always well, and certainly not always with the amount of patience and perspective or consistency we'd like. But we do it.

. . .

A few weeks after we made the big transition to underpants, another big transition was happening elsewhere in my family: my brother and his wife, who lived in Portland, Maine, gave birth to their son, my nephew.

I drove up to see him a few days after he was born, and a few weeks after that we went up as a family, staying with my parents. The girls were sweetly curious and eager to interact with their new cousin—Elsa especially. (No honey, you can't put that stuffed animal onto him like that. No, sweetie, you can't feed him a cracker.)

In the evening, my brother and his wife went out for a few hours while my mother and I took care of the baby. I was reminded of how bewildering it is to try to decode a baby's cries. Is he hungry? Does he need a new diaper? Is he gassy? Just tired? Lord knows I never knew for sure with the girls when they were newborns. (And I should add that holding my nephew—warm and cute and sweet-smelling as he was—I felt not even the slightest ovarian twinge.)

But I was also reminded that, as challenging as the first year was for me, it was also something of a honeymoon: Look at me! I'm a mom! I've got babies! Isn't this crazy? It's crazy! I suppose it helped that I wasn't at all depressed during that period. Exhausted and stressed out sometimes, yes. But never chemically, clinically down.

And as I walked around that night with my tiny nephew, bouncing and shushing to get him to settle down while simultaneously trying not to trip over the toys and crayons and books Elsa and Clio had left scattered on the rug, it hit me in a sudden and visceral way: I didn't have babies anymore; I had children. I'd ceased to be a new mother. I was a *parent* now.

It was one of those rare moments in life where you're suddenly able to look back at the distance you've traveled, keeping your head down and eyes on the path the whole time, and realize: Whoah. I've gotten myself to a completely different place.

Being a mother had gone from a novelty to an ingrained part of who I was. I was growing steadily more confident in my mothering abilities, and was starting to get to know my girls as the people they were becoming. I ached to be more present for them, both emotionally and in terms of hours spent with them.

Yet at the same time, I grieved, deeply, something that I'd had before my children were born that I'd lost along the way: a sense of confidence, drive, and direction in my writing—the feeling that I *was* a writer, as opposed to someone who'd tried and failed and was now too busy and dispirited to have another go at it.

And my job had obviously lost its appeal, in part because I was spending more time at it, but probably also because I'd been there for five years and needed a change of scene and pace.

I needed to recalibrate—to reconcile the various elements of my life and my sense of self in a way that I could sustain going forward. And getting my brain chemistry back in check was a key piece of that puzzle.

Not long after that, I told my psychiatrist that I'd had enough; the new medication he had added to my cocktail two months earlier didn't seem to be doing anything. We had to try something else; I couldn't go on like this.

He decided to try adding a low dose of an antidepressant to my regimen. And within a few weeks, it felt as if sunshine was finding its way through the cracks in the walls around me. And as the light grew steadily brighter, my resolve to make a life change blossomed.

22

I've enjoyed your writing in this forum for some time but lately have not found myself persuaded by or remotely sympathetic to the "dilemmas" you present.

I suspect that I am starting to be entirely overwhelmed by the chorus of privileged, complaining women about the disconnect between home and work and the "utter" difficulty of "having it all."

This is part of a comment by a first-name-only reader in response to a post on my blog where I wrote about the frustration of trying to achieve a balance of work and writing and spending time with the girls, with the added complication of a mood disorder.

The commenter explained that it was all quite simple, and at this point in the "national discussion" on the topic we should all understand the repercussions of our choices: Women who want to be with their children during their "fleeting" infancy and early childhood have to sacrifice their demanding work schedules. On the other hand, women who choose to continue pursuing their careers have to accept that it's at the expense of spending more time with their families.

She closed, kindly, by writing:

Even with a voice as witty and talented as yours, the incessant whining (much like a toddler's) is unattractive and unbecoming, especially in your relatively privileged circumstance.

After reading through it a few times, once my hands had stopped shaking and I drafted the response I *didn't* plan to post—the one full of expletives and rage—I composed the most measured response I could muster. I said that, yes, women today are quite aware of the consequences and sacrifices inherent in their choices. But that doesn't make those choices any easier to make, and many women—myself included—find it helpful to discuss these dilemmas with other women puzzling through the same challenges. (And I did congratulate her at the end for having figured it all out. Because I couldn't help getting in a little dig.)

I don't know one woman—except for my charming anonymous commenter—who doesn't struggle at times with the push and pull of children and work and spouse and self—not to mention the dreams and passions that fall outside the realm of simple logistic possibility. And what of trying to be a good partner/friend/daughter/sister/neighbor, to stay healthy and reasonably fit, and—while we're at it—to get involved in your community/school/church/etc.?

More to the point, how do we decide which of these pieces to keep, which ones to put on the back burner, and which ones to let go of altogether? What if we make the wrong choices and regret them for the rest of our lives?

When I was a senior in college, returning after a semester in Africa and a turbulent summer during which Alastair and I semi–broke up, I spent the first weeks of the semester frantically dropping and signing up for courses, totally bewildered as to which ones I should take. It was eating me up inside, keeping me awake at night with anxiety. At some point in this process, while trying to change a class after the regular "drop-add" period, I had to get a signature from my academic advisor—a religion professor and Unitarian minister who oozed wisdom and serenity. She asked me what, exactly, was going on. Why all the indecision? At which point I broke down in tears.

"You're *overwhelmed*," she said, once I'd stopped blabbing and blubbering. "You've seen the world beyond college. You've got a major relationship in transition. You're about to graduate. You're over*whelmed!*"

I'm pretty sure she also used the "f" word at some point in our conversation, along the lines of ". . . it doesn't fucking matter whether you take American Lit or Music History as your fourth course, I promise," which made her seem instantly, like, even cooler. (And made me do that weird laugh/cry thing, where you laugh and it makes you cry harder.)

Overwhelmed was exactly what I was now, nearly fifteen years later, with my almost three-year-old, very spirited twins; a nearly full-time job that I didn't want to be at; a nearly defeated writer self; and nearly incapacitating depression.

But my snarky blog-commenter friend was right on one count: I am quite privileged. Not only do my husband and I have college educations and a financial safety net, thanks to our parents, I also have a vocation, copywriting, that pays well and is possible to do on a part-time or freelance basis. I also have a husband who is willing and able to do the lion's share of weekday childcare, on account of his own peculiar profession.

That husband is also amazingly supportive. And when I was

wrestling with whether or not to leave my job and try freelancing, he was 100 percent behind my making the leap. To my fears that we'd end up in the poorhouse, he said that, on the contrary, he thought I was more likely to have *too* much work and not get my writing done as a result.

"Look," he said, "think of it as an experiment. You try it for a year, maybe two, and if it doesn't work, you'll find a full-time job."

We must have had the "I want to freelance but it would be crazy, right?" conversation several dozen times that fall. The poor guy. But he never wavered. Do it, he said. You can do it. We'll be fine.

By mid-November, I had made up my mind.

I told my best friends first, and then my parents. Doing this made it feel more real, more possible. More exciting. Now I started worrying that once I felt better—once the depression had lifted completely, as it was well on its way to doing—I'd start feeling like everything was fine as it was, hunky-dory, and change my mind. And I didn't *want* to change my mind.

But the better I felt, the better I felt about my decision. I gave my notice at work in early December. Two months later, I'd be out on my own.

Just a few days after I gave notice, we got the first snow of the season—wet stuff, not destined to last, but enough that we still had to put on boots to tromp about. We decided, on a lark, and suffering from a touch of cabin fever, to take a drive with the girls up to Marblehead—the same quaint ocean-side town to which Alastair and I had gone for a spontaneous day trip almost exactly three years earlier, although neither of us realized the coincidence until we were on the way back home. We had no plan except to walk around, look at the ocean, and maybe get some lunch.

During the drive up, Alastair and I were talking about this and that. Work, family, the nuclear-test-ban treaty, who knows? Every once in a while, as we were driving, one of the girls would ask, apropos of nothing, "Are you talking about my birthday?" They knew that their birthdays were coming up soon, so it was a hot topic of conversation. (And as far as they were concerned, what else could we possibly be talking about?)

At one point, I was laughing at something Alastair said, and Elsa asked, "Mommy, why are you laughing?"

I told her that Daddy was very silly, and he said lots of funny things.

"Yeah?" she said. She was quiet for a little while, and Alastair and I continued in whatever silly vein of conversation we'd been in. But the next time I laughed, Elsa laughed, too. Just because it was clearly the thing to do.

It made me realize that, whereas we once were able to converse freely in front of the girls without them really even registering it, we were moving into quite a different phase now. They were ever more keenly aware of what people around them were saying. Our front-seat conversations were no longer as private as they once were. We couldn't talk about the girls and expect them not to hear or understand.

Later on our outing, after having lunch at a place by the water that was really beyond the budget of an about-to-be-completely-self-employed household, the girls stomped on iced-over puddles and played with handfuls of snow at a boat landing near the edge of the water. We watched their delighted explorations for a few minutes, and then I made a snowball, which I lobbed at Alastair.

He threw one back at me, harder. And I called him a jerk and playfully tossed some snow back at him. It was the sort of silly, flirty horseplay we've done throughout the course of our very long relationship. Natural as breathing to us.

Except now we had an audience: before we knew it, Elsa was flinging snow—rather hard, crusty, icy snow—at both of us, thinking it was the funniest thing in the world. Alastair got a good whack in the face at one point. And we felt like idiots, because it's pretty hard to turn around and say, "snow isn't for throwing at people!" when, as you've just demonstrated, it clearly is.

"Look at us," I said. "We're supposed to be setting an example."

"We are," he said. "Just not a very good one."

But at least we were having fun with each other. In spite of just having spent more money than we wanted to in a restaurant full of mostly older people, the majority of whom seemed less than pleased to be sharing their Sunday brunch with two admittedly cute but also very, very loud children (remember: dining out with twin toddlers = almost never a good idea). In spite of the day-to-day stress and craziness and exhaustion of our lives, and the uncertainty that lay ahead. In spite of it all, we could still relax and smile and love each other. Which, in the grand scheme of parental example setting, has to count for something, right?

I also like to think that, by doing my damnedest to get over my depression and going after the life I want, risks and all, I've set a pretty decent example for my children. But I guess the jury will be out on that one for quite some time.

They say that the first three years with twins are the hardest. And that sounds about right to me.

It wasn't as if everything became dramatically easier as the girls approached and then surpassed the three-year mark. There were (and are) still tantrums and whining and the emotional exhaustion of trying to meet two competing sets of similar needs and wants at exactly the same time. The sibling rivalry arguably worsened. And on the flip side, the girls learned to conspire together: bedtime became even more challenging when, after lights-out, they consulted each other on what their next move would be.

I eavesdropped on several such conversations, like one that occurred when we were staying at Alastair's parents' house over Thanksgiving, and having a helluva time getting the girls to stay in their room:

> **Clio:** Are you going to get out of bed?
> **Elsa:** Yeah.
> **Clio:** Turn on the light!
> **Elsa:** OK. (pause) The door is locked!
> > (Unbeknownst to them, I was standing at the door, holding it shut, in hopes of foiling their escape.)
> **Clio:** Say you need to go poopies.
> > (It's quite clear who the brains behind this sort of operation were.)
> **Elsa:** Mommy! I got poopies!!

But their cleverness had an upside as well (in addition to comedic value): they became steadily more independent and self-sufficient. I remember my panic at the realization that Elsa could open the refrigerator on her own—is she going to be going in there and pulling things off the shelves at random? leaving the door open and running up our electric bills?—turning soon to delight: she actually understood and obeyed us when we explained that she could not take anything out of the fridge without asking. And, even better, she could now go and get her milk or water cup on her own if she was thirsty. One less thing we had to do!

Clio's freak-outs over control lessened in frequency and intensity. Meltdowns from either of the girls became easier to head off, partly because we had learned how to play defense and stand firm. But also because the girls' comprehension and capacity for reason had increased so measurably. They were still irrational plenty of the time. But at least we had the sense that they were operating in the same general galaxy of logic as us.

They asked questions (frequently about things I couldn't adequately answer—e.g., "Mommy, why is pee yellow?" Umm . . .). They began to say, "I love you," and give us hugs and kisses, unprompted. And they created and lost themselves in adorably bizarre and imaginative pretend play scenarios, some of which they invited us in on:

"Lie on the couch!" they commanded me one morning. "We're going to fix you!"

"Fix me how?"

"Come see!" My curiosity and my delight at their initiative won out over my reluctance to abandon my coffee and the magazine article I was reading, so I obeyed.

Clio sat beside me and patted my hand and said, "It's going to be OK," while Elsa retrieved their play doctor kit. The two of them then proceeded to "fix" each part of me: Elsa used the stethoscope to listen to my stomach, while Clio used the thermometer to look into my ears. They applied the blood pressure cuff to my feet and tapped my head gently with the reflex hammer.

"There," Elsa said when they were all done.

"How do you feel?" asked Clio.

"I feel great," I told them.

And I truly did.

Recovering from my depression and subsequently leaving my job felt at once like a homecoming and the start of a new adventure. I had myself—my confidence, my humor, my ordinary contentment—back. And I had the chance to try to shape a new life—one that made more sense for who I was and what mattered most to me.

When I first left work and was at home more of the time, the girls were thrown for a loop, the way young kids often are when their regular routine is disrupted. They were clingy and cranky, and definitely did not understand the work-at-home concept. *But Mommy's home! Right up there in her office! So why can't we go see her and play with her? Why can't she come kiss my boo-boo when I get hurt?* I quickly learned that in order to get anything done, I had to leave the house, so now I divide my time between various local coffee shops.

Sometimes I get really, really sick of coffee and tea. But it's far better than having to drive in to an office every day, fighting traffic in both directions. And now, the girls are adjusted to the new routine: I take them to school in the mornings and stop work at five thirty sharp to play with them and make dinner. If I'm around, I can take a break to put them down for their "quiet time" after lunch, or wipe the occasional butt. I'm part of their everyday lives—beyond just bedtime. I love it. And I feel so damned lucky.

The freelance projects started slowly, but gradually grew in frequency and scope. I had a steady stream of work and—as Alastair predicted—frequently more than I could handle. Meanwhile, my fiction and nonfiction writing went from the far back burner to the front. Granted, still the burner on the left—the one where you cook the rice, as opposed to the burner where you put the big twelve-inch skillet for the main course. Copywriting was still the meat, in terms of hours and certainly in terms of income. But at least now I had rice. You gotta have rice. (You're holding some of it in your hands, actually. Hope you like rice.)

And just before I left my job, I found a small co-op press that wanted to publish my novel. Not the big New York–press novel debut I'd hoped for; but I'd moved on from that dream. I just wanted people to read the book.

And the depression? I've had a few mood valleys since climbing up from the down-deep D-hole, but they've been short-lived and shallow. Nothing like the debilitating episodes of the two previous years. As for peaks, those happen sometimes, too. But they're more like foothills.

The various parts of my life and my identity coexist in harmony now. They even overlap: I write about my children (the rice you're still holding), something I never imagined I'd do back when I was at the Iowa Writers' Workshop. But something I've found immensely rewarding.

I am a mother. I am a writer. I am an independent professional.

This harmony may well revert to cacophony once again when another great change (or two, or three) whips through my life. I will have to recalibrate once again. Maybe sooner than I'd like.

But I also realize now—as I think all mothers, twin or otherwise, come to realize—that the feeling that there's more noise, more frustration, more work, more chaos, more stress, and more *everything* than I can gracefully and seamlessly handle is an inherent part of motherhood. There will always be times when I am strained by the burden, and when the constant effort of it feels like too much. But there will also always be moments of joy that make it worth the trouble.

As I write this, I am healthy. I am happy. I have an incredible husband. And I have two smart, spirited, LOUD, and beautiful daughters whom I love more and more each day. To say that I'm doubly blessed by their presence in my life doesn't even begin to cut it.

Acknowledgments

A double helping of thanks to the wonderful people who helped bring this project to fruition: Henry Dunow, agent and father of twins extraordinaire; Nichole Argyres and Laura Chasen at St. Martin's Press; Jami Brandli, Eve Bridburg, Rebecca Morgan Frank, Ellen Litman, Jessica Murphy Moo, and Heidi Pitlor, all of whom provided invaluable feedback and suggestions along the way; and Preston Browning and his magical Wellspring House, where a good chunk of this book was written. Extra special thanks to my *Baby Squared* blog readers, whose virtual friendship and support has been a treasured part of my parenting journey. Most of all, my love and gratitude to Alastair, the best companion on this big adventure that a gal could ever hope for.